SCOTLAND

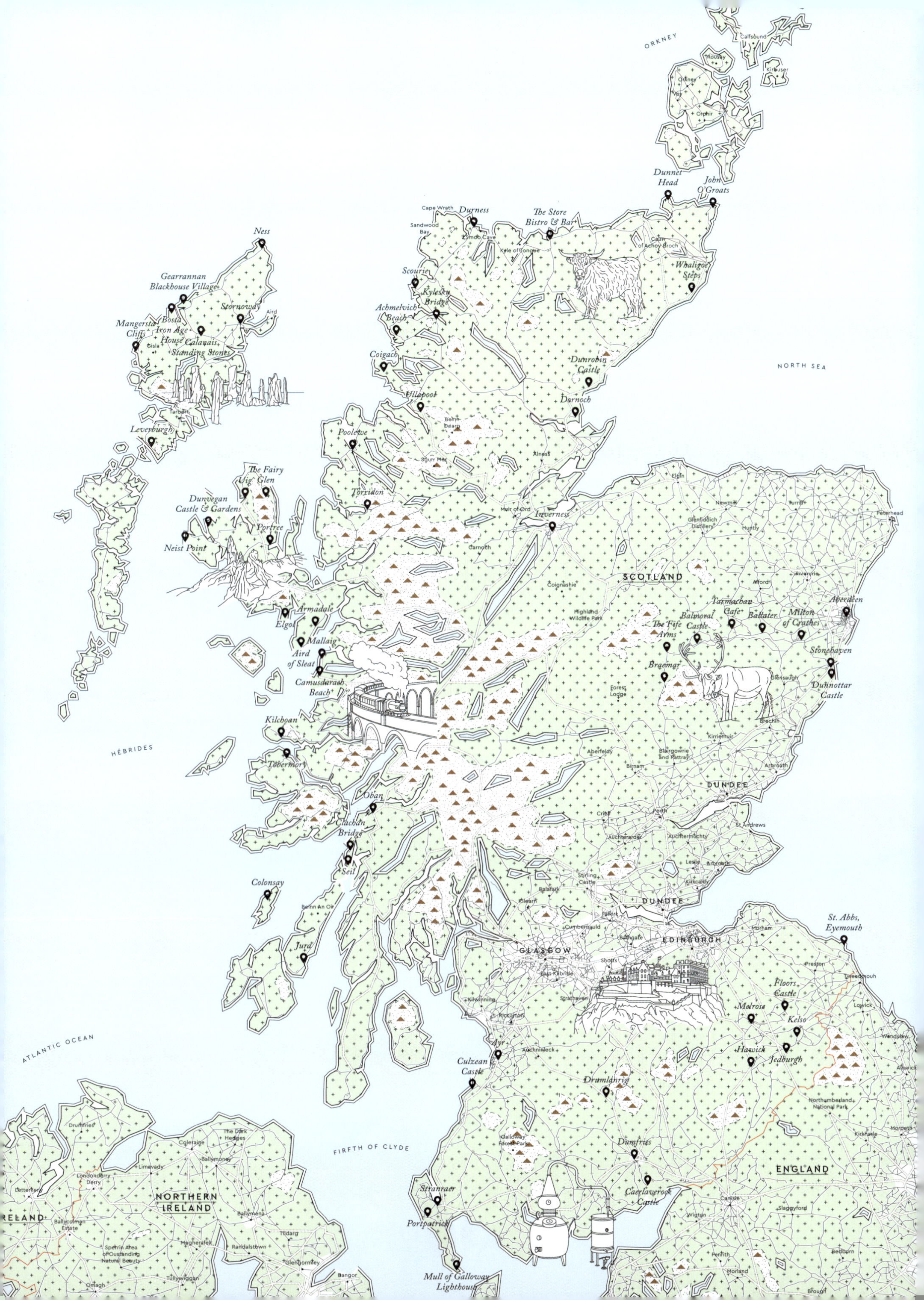

ORKNEY
Calfsound
Rousay
Kirbuster
Orkney
Orphir
Dunnet Head
John O'Groats
Cape Wrath
Durness
Sandwood Bay
Smoo Cave
The Store Bistro & Bar
Kyle of Tongue
Cairn of Achoy Broch
Whaligoe Steps
Ness
Gearrannan Blackhouse Village
Stornoway
Aird
Bosta Iron Age House
Mangersta Cliffs
Gisla
Calanais Standing Stones
Tarbert
Leverburgh
Scourie
Kylesku Bridge
Achmelvich Beach
Coigach
Dunrobin Castle
NORTH SEA
Ullapool
Dornoch
Beinn Dearg
Poolewe
Sgurr Mor
Alness
The Fairy Glen
Uig
Dunvegan Castle & Gardens
Portree
Neist Point
Torridon
Elgin
Newmill
Burrifi
Peterhead
Muir of Ord
Inverness
Glenfiddich Distillery
Huntly
Carnoch
SCOTLAND
Inverurie
Alford
Coignashie
Aberdeen
Armadale
Elgol
Highland Wildlife Park
Tarmachan Cafe
Balmoral Castle
Ballater
Milton of Crathes
The Fife Arms
Mallaig
Aird of Sleat
Braemar
Stonehaven
Camusdarach Beach
Glensaugh
Dunnottar Castle
Forest Lodge
Brechin
Kilchoan
HÉBRIDES
Kirriemuir
Tobermory
Aberfeldy
Blairgowrie and Rattray
Birnam
Arbroath
DUNDEE
Oban
Crieff
Perth
St Andrews
Clachan Bridge
Auchterarder
Auchtermuchty
Seil
Leslie
Stirling Castle
Kirkcaldy
Colonsay
Balafark
Killearn
DUNDEE
Beinn An Oir
Falkirk
Cumbernauld
Bathgate
Morham
St. Abbs, Eyemouth
Jura
GLASGOW
EDINBURGH
Shotts
East Kilbride
Preston
Floors Castle
Strathaven
Kilwinning
Melrose
Kelso
ATLANTIC OCEAN
Ayr
Auchinleck
Hawick
Jedburgh
Culzean Castle
Drumlanrig
Northumberland National Park
Galloway Forest Park
Morpeth
Kielder
FIRTH OF CLYDE
Dumfries
Limavady
Coleraine
The Dark Hedges
Ballymoney
Londonderry Derry
Letterkenny
ENGLAND
Stranraer
Caerlaverock Castle
NORTHERN IRELAND
Carlisle
Slaggyford
IRELAND
Ballycolman Estate
Ballymena
Portpatrick
Wigton
Magherafelt
Sperrin Area of Outstanding Natural Beauty
Randalstown
Penrith
Bedburn
Glengormley
Morland
Mull of Galloway Lighthouse
Bangor
Tullywiggan
Omagh

THE EXTRAORDINARY GUIDES

SCOTLAND

MAUD SIMON

RIZZOLI UNIVERSE

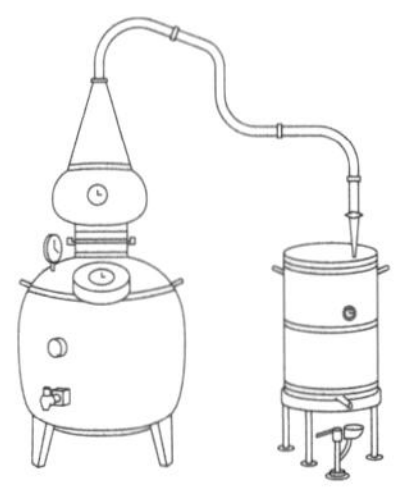

INTRODUCTION

Scotland is a territory whose borders defy land and sea. More than seven hundred and ninety islands are dotted around its coastline (ninety-three of which are inhabited), divided between four major archipelagos: Shetland, Orkney, and the Inner and Outer Hebrides. Lying between the Atlantic Ocean and the North Sea, Scotland's rich and eventful history stretches back to the Paleolithic era and while it is impossible to summarize its entire past in this short introduction, certain events have certainly played a part. The Picts, the Scots (a Celtic tribe), and the Vikings all left their mark on Scotland, and their presence can still be discerned in place names from Ben Macdui (Gaelic) and Orkney (Old Norse) to Aberdeen (Pictish).

The Picts and Scots united in the Middle Ages to found Alba, the future kingdom of Scotland. Robert the Bruce became king in 1306 and led the struggle for his country's independence, with success sealed by his victory over the armies of Edward II, the king of England, at the Battle of Bannockburn in 1314. The ruins of castles scattered across the landscape are a reminder of the rivalry between the two crowns.

James Stuart, James VI of Scotland, succeeded to the thrones of England and Scotland in 1603 as James I, uniting the two crowns. A century later the 1707 Act of Union created the kingdom of Great Britain, resulting in the dissolution of the Scottish Parliament in favor of the assembly in Westminster and unleashing further tension. The Jacobite risings to bring about the restoration of the Stuart dynasty against the Protestant monarchy began in 1689, with support from the Highland clans. The rebellion was finally put down in 1746, at the bloody Battle of Culloden, a defeat that paved the way for the Highland Clearances. Clan society was crushed, the inhabitants of the Highlands and Western Isles were forced into exile, and the countryside was cleared for sheep farming.

Despite all this, nothing could erase Scottish identity, which survived in language, traditions, poetry, music, legends, and, of course, in literature. Tartan, the checkered pattern that is the symbol of the clans, was banned after the Jacobite risings, but the ban was lifted in 1782 and tartan is ubiquitous in Scotland today. In terms of language, Scottish Gaelic and Scots (closely related to English) have taken their place alongside English as the three official languages of the country. Bolstered by this unique identity, Scotland entered a new era with the reestablishment of its parliament in 1999 and, although the referendum of 2014 kept the country within the United Kingdom for the moment, the question of independence still lingers.

From the Lowlands to the remote Shetlands, and from the rugged scenery of the Highlands to the sun-kissed islands of the Hebrides, Scotland finds an echo of its history in the power of its landscape—a wild epic that no traveler will ever forget.

A VOLCANIC CAPITAL

IN AND AROUND
EDINBURGH

The city of Edinburgh is built on ancient volcanic hills. Although listed as a UNESCO World Heritage Site, a bustling, modern city lurks behind its museums and neoclassical facades.

P. 8

Edinburgh is a vibrant city built on ancient volcanic hills.

OPPOSITE

Edinburgh was designated the world's first UNESCO City of Literature in 2004.

"Half a capital and half a country town, the whole city leads a double existence; it has long trances of the one and flashes of the other; like the king of the Black Isles, it is half alive and half a monumental marble." In his essay *Edinburgh: Picturesque Notes*, Robert Louis Stevenson sums up the spirit of the Scottish capital perfectly as a museum-city that is eternally alive and in motion.

This duality is similarly reflected in its topography. Edinburgh was built on ancient volcanic hills (the most notable of which is named Arthur's Seat) and is divided in two: the historic medieval center, with its narrow, picturesque streets, lies to the south, while the elegant Georgian buildings of New Town, laid out according to Enlightenment ideals, are to the north. Its ubiquitous cafés, galleries, pubs, and independent stores have created a vibrant city where one minute the visitor can be in a gallery gazing at paintings by Rubens or Sir Henry Raeburn and the next whiling away an hour or so on the terrace of a fashionable café rereading classic works by Robert Louis Stevenson (*The Strange Case of Dr. Jekyll and Mr. Hyde*), Sir Walter Scott (*Ivanhoe*), or Arthur Conan Doyle (any number of Sherlock Holmes tales).

The city's name dates back to the seventh century, when the town was known as Eidyn Burh; *burh* means "fortress," and the castle still dominates the skyline. The Royal Mile is the street that runs down from this stronghold to the Palace of Holyroodhouse, an official royal residence that is a link between the ancient and modern history of the city. Nearby is the pride of Scotland, the Scottish Parliament building, which opened in 2004 as part of the British policy of devolution, and gave a voice to an entire nation.

Edinburgh has one foot firmly planted in the modern world and transforms each summer into an open-air theater when the Edinburgh Festival Fringe takes over the entire city, attracting crowds from all over the world. This is when those seeking peace and quiet need to take refuge in the quieter outskirts of the city, or to get out of it entirely. The green valleys of the Scottish Borders stretch away to the south of Edinburgh, sheltering magnificent abbeys and rural hamlets in which the first tweeds were woven. To the north, the coast road winds its way from port to port along the Fife Peninsula until reaching the pretty town of St Andrews, home to both the first university founded in Scotland and the country's most famous golf course.

THE ESSENTIALS

01

MELROSE ABBEY

This pink stone abbey was founded on the orders of King David I in 1137. The heart of Robert the Bruce is said to lie buried here.

02

THE SCOTT MONUMENT

This Gothic monument, more than 200 ft (61 m) high, was erected to the memory of the writer Sir Walter Scott, the author of such notable works as *Ivanhoe*.

03

EDINBURGH CASTLE

Construction of this medieval fortress, which still dominates the city's skyline to this day, began in the eleventh century.

04

CALTON HILL

Edinburgh's version of the Acropolis in Athens was built in a neoclassical style on top of this volcanic hill to the east of Princes Street.

05

SCOTTISH NATIONAL PORTRAIT GALLERY

An impressive collection of portraits has been on display in this magnificent red sandstone Gothic Revival gallery since 1889.

06

DEAN VILLAGE

Once home to a community of millers, this picturesque, green refuge on the banks of the Water of Leith is a stone's throw from the hustle and bustle of the city.

07

PRINCES STREET GARDENS

This extensive park in the heart of the city offers some of the most beautiful views of the monuments that surround it.

08

NATIONAL GALLERY OF SCOTLAND

A museum housing a host of painting masterpieces, from Leonardo da Vinci to Velázquez, by way of Gauguin and Rubens.

09

CIRCUS LANE

This charming cobbled mews, which resembles a film set, was once lined with stables.

10

NATIONAL MUSEUM OF SCOTLAND

There's an element of a cabinet of curiosities to this museum with its glazed roof beneath which are collections that span geology, the decorative arts, science, and technology.

11

PALACE OF HOLYROODHOUSE

The British monarchy's official Edinburgh residence is open to the public apart from during royal visits. The ruins of a majestic abbey stand in its grounds.

12

ARTHUR'S SEAT

This ancient volcano overlooking the city is the perfect place to stride across heather and moorland while admiring Edinburgh from a high vantage point.

ABOVE

Nature is found everywhere, even among the charming terraced stone buildings.

OPPOSITE

Climb the ancient hill of Arthur's Seat for a breathtaking view.

ABOVE

Victoria Street in the historic center of the city is known for its colorful houses.

OPPOSITE

Taking a break within the walls of Edinburgh Castle, perched high on a hill overlooking the city.

ARTS AND CRAFTS

AULD ALLIANCE KILTMAKERS

THE ART OF BESPOKE KILTMAKING

Two French tailors have settled in Edinburgh and make kilts entirely by hand, helping to save this icon of Scottish heritage threatened by the disappearance of independent kiltmakers.

Mathilde and Jonathan's workshop is discreetly tucked away in their apartment, which is located at the far end of Holyrood Park. They left their native Burgundy in 2018 to put down roots in the Scottish capital with a single objective in mind: to learn how to make a kilt. Having been enchanted by tailoring since high school, the couple had discovered the city the previous year when visiting tartan weaving mills. Charmed by this traditional skill with its strong roots in local culture, they decided to learn the "rules of the game" (as they like to put it) but found it difficult to find training. And no wonder—there are practically no training courses left and the craft was added to the Heritage Crafts Association's (HCA) list as one of the skills in danger of dying out. The profession survives only through a handful of independent kiltmakers to whom Mathilde and Jonathan turned before striking out on their own. The name of the company was to be "Auld Alliance Kiltmakers," a reference to the pact forged between the kingdoms of France and Scotland in the late thirteenth century.

The workshop is like an Aladdin's cave of the kilts that Mathilde and Jonathan sew by hand. Large binders contain samples from the tartan collections of the country's major weavers (Marton Mills, Andrew Elliot, and, of course, Lochcarron of Scotland) much beloved of high-end designer Vivienne Westwood and haute couture houses such as Burberry, Chanel, and Dior.

During the first fitting, a client browses through the pattern books to find a tartan that best suits their purpose and preference. The majority of tartans are listed in the Scottish Register of Tartans, which keeps a record of their "recipe" (the threadcount for each color) and preserves their history. Mathilde and Jonathan also offer customers the option to create their own tartan, which is then woven by one of the country's textile mills.

Once the tartan is chosen, the next step is to select the style of pleating, which brings the pattern to life, and to choose a color for the leather straps that hold the kilt in place. The client's measurements are taken for fit. During the three to four months required to make the kilt, photos are regularly sent to its future owner to show what is happening behind the scenes. "This allows us to share small details that will no longer be visible once the kilt is finished, such as little mottos or messages sewn into the lining," explains Jonathan. The final fitting is always an emotional moment. "Until the final fitting the bottom of the pleats are held in place with white thread," adds Mathilde. "The moment we pull it out to reveal the way the pleats move is always magical."

MATHILDE AND JONATHAN

The couple maintain a healthy respect for Scottish craftsmanship while adding their own modern touch.

SCOTTISH WEAVERS

Collections of tartans from the country's major textile weavers are stored in thick sample books.

ABOVE

The motto of this well-known artisan bakery is "Simple things made well."

OPPOSITE

There's a certain symmetry to the architecture of Queen Street.

ABOVE

A bagpipe player in Princes Street.

OPPOSITE

A view of Edinburgh's Old Town from Princes Street Gardens.

CULTURE

THE MUSEUMS OF EDINBURGH

NATIONAL MUSEUM OF SCOTLAND

The museum's Grand Gallery is housed in a light-filled atrium. The museum is one of the most fascinating in the country, housing displays from the worlds of nature, the sciences, the decorative arts, and the history of Scotland.

NATIONAL GALLERY OF SCOTLAND

Dedicated to painting, this museum houses any number of masterpieces.

SCOTTISH NATIONAL PORTRAIT GALLERY

A museum dedicated to portraiture, both on canvas and in photographs.

THE WRITERS' MUSEUM

The place to see manuscripts by Robert Burns, Sir Walter Scott, and Robert Louis Stevenson, among many others.

SCOTTISH STORYTELLING CENTRE

The Scottish art of storytelling is celebrated in this medieval building.

NATIONAL MUSEUM OF SCOTLAND

The Todhead Lighthouse lantern has been preserved and rebuilt in the main gallery of the museum.

SURGEONS' HALL MUSEUMS

The Royal College of Surgeons was founded in 1505. The museum chronicles surgical pathology and the use of medical instruments.

ST CECILIA'S HALL

Home to one of the most beautiful collections of musical instruments in the country.

SURGEONS' HALL MUSEUMS

The original purpose of this museum was to teach medical students.

A panoramic view of Edinburgh from the castle, perched on the slopes of an extinct volcano.

DEEP DIVE

THE FORTH BRIDGE

With its monumental arches and striking red framework, the Forth Bridge is the very incarnation of the boldness of Scottish industry, and has left its mark on the landscape and the imagination of the country for more than a century.

The bridge was opened in 1890 and crosses the Firth of Forth between the villages of South Queensferry and North Queensferry. It carries the Edinburgh–Aberdeen railway line and was seen as an unparalleled feat of engineering from the moment of its inauguration. A mile and a half (2.5 km) in length, it features three giant cantilevers resting on piers, a solution that was unprecedented at the time and that allows the bridge to span the estuary without a central support and to absorb the mechanical stresses caused by winds and tides.

The bridge's construction came at a pivotal moment in the history of British engineering (in the wake of the Tay Bridge disaster of 1879). Methods for calculating strength and load bearing were evolving, with safety becoming a major concern, and steel, a material that was still relatively new when used on this scale, proved to be the cornerstone of the project. The large, specialized workforce engaged for the bridge's construction was employed for several years, painstakingly assembling every element of a structure that had been designed to last.

Designed to withstand winds in excess of 93 mph (150 km/h), the bridge is a massive presence in the landscape and its now iconic dark-red color was the result of a practical choice—the red paint is a protective coating intended to slow down the corrosion caused by the salty air. Although it soon became synonymous with an endless task (prompting the popular expression "It's like painting the Forth Bridge"), the task of maintaining the structure's fabric has since been modernized but without ever having to interrupt the bridge's operation.

Listed as a UNESCO World Heritage Site in 2015, the Forth Bridge remains a major rail link and a familiar landmark of the Scottish countryside. From the waterfront at South Queensferry, the bridge stands out against the estuary and is visible for miles around. It has been photographed, painted, and filmed, becoming a recurrent motif in the visual culture of the area and, for more than a century, a constant companion in the daily lives of locals and visitors alike.

Crossing the bridge from the Edinburgh side also marks a transition to the more open land of the north, making crossing the Firth of Forth both a functional yet also a special experience, like crossing a border. Still in use today, the Forth Bridge is no isolated monument; it is a living piece of architecture, a structure where technical ingenuity has become a permanent part of the landscape but without altering its setting.

FROM DRAWING BOARD TO FINAL STRUCTURE

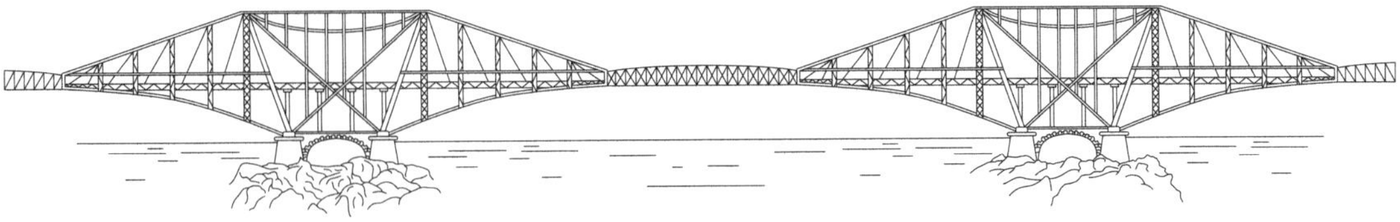

1 / PRELIMINARY PLAN

A version based on a cantilevered structure designed to span the estuary and spread the load with no intermediate support.

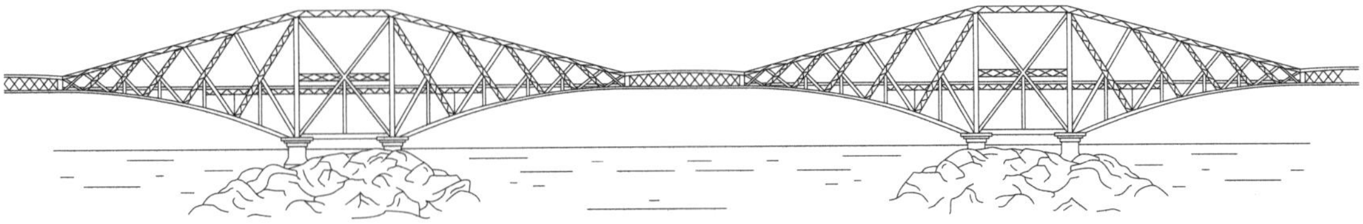

2 / FINAL PLAN

The final version selected for the project, with a streamlined metal frame to improve stability, span, and wind resistance.

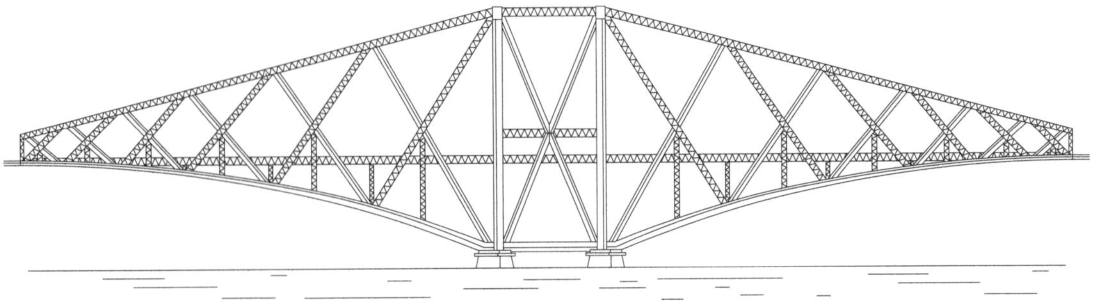

3 / DETAIL

A close-up view of the arrangement of steel trusses designed to absorb mechanical stress, distribute the weight of rail traffic, and resist climatic influences.

STRUCTURAL PRINCIPLE

The Forth Bridge is based on a system of interlinked cantilevers, with steel trusses to transmit loads to the three main piers.

ABOVE

Edinburgh's architecture seen from one of the rooms of No.11 Hotel.

OPPOSITE

Inner courtyards and flower gardens lie hidden away behind the heavy stone facades.

BACK TO THE LAND

THE FREE COMPANY

FROM FARM TO FORK

The Free Company, founded by brothers Angus and Charlie Buchanan-Smith among the ridges of the Pentland Hills to the south of Edinburgh, wears many hats. It is simultaneously an organic farm, a seasonal restaurant, and a space for the sharing of knowledge, a place where the expression "farm to table" applies in every sense.

Despite what traditional wisdom might claim, the grass is sometimes greener on *this* side of the fence, which is certainly the case with the fields of the Free Company's farm, which lies around a thousand feet (300 m) below the surrounding uplands. The top-quality pasture here, which is perfect for feeding livestock, did not escape the notice of the University of Edinburgh's Department of Agriculture, who decided to buy the property at the end of the nineteenth century. Fifty years later, when the owners decided to move their activities to the other side of the hill, Professor Alick Buchanan-Smith decided to stay on.

For the next eighty years, the family farm was given over to raising a herd of Ayrshire dairy cows (a squat, local breed perfectly adapted to Scotland's fickle climate) and the business flourished until the turn of the millennium, when a drop in milk prices forced it to cease production and scale back its activity. Its future hanging in the balance, things took a new turn for the farm with the involvement in 2016 of Angus and Charlie, Alick's grandsons, and two of their friends. And what did they have in mind? No less than to regenerate the farm with a scheme that would add a restaurant to the estate, featuring a menu based on its produce. A kitchen garden and greenhouses would produce organic vegetables while sheep, pigs, and rare heritage cattle would roam the fields. The old stables were converted into a restaurant with a communal table seating up to eighty covers, and the whole undertaking has proved a roaring success. Reservations are essential, and every dinner begins with cocktails in the gardens where it all began, as the farm's produce really does dictate what's on the menu. Diners are encouraged to ask questions to find out about how the farm operates and there is an introductory presentation explaining regenerative agriculture, pasture management, crop rotation, and local breed selection. Everything here is designed to be a teachable moment, reflecting the operation's roots—the desire to share knowledge has never faded. Angus and Charlie are now realizing their dream of making the Free Company a sustainable and desirable model that flies in the face of industrial logic—a place where you come for dinner but leave transformed.

1 / 3 / A BAND OF BROTHERS

Brothers Angus and Charlie Buchanan-Smith are together writing the next chapter in the story of their family farm.

2 / REGENERATIVE AGRICULTURE

With The Free Company, Angus and Charlie are trying to show that other methods of agricultural production are possible.

4 / TRANSMISSION OF IDEAS

The garden, where it all began, lies at the heart of every meal and workshop, where the two brothers share what they have learned on the land with as many people as possible.

ABOVE

The Union Canal runs for 30 miles (50 km) between Falkirk and the heart of Edinburgh.

OPPOSITE

There are views over the canal and local houses from some of the rooms in the family-run Bridge Inn in the village of Ratho.

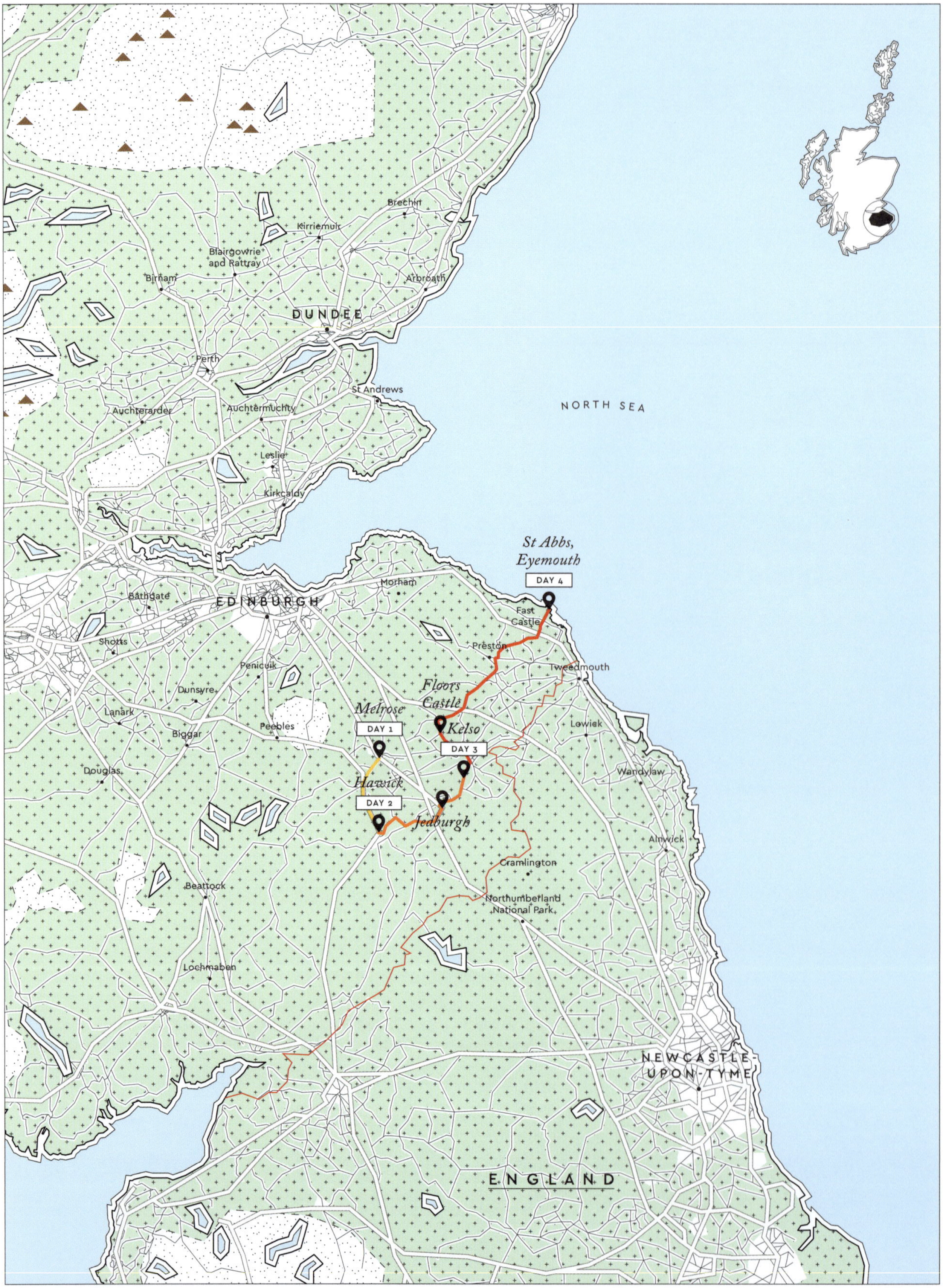
Brechin
Kirriemuir
Blairgowrie and Rattray
Birnam
Arbroath
DUNDEE
Perth
St Andrews
Auchterarder
Auchtermuchty
NORTH SEA
Leslie
Kirkcaldy
St Abbs, Eyemouth
DAY 4
Morham
Bathgate
EDINBURGH
Fast Castle
Shotts
Preston
Penicuik
Tweedmouth
Dunsyre
Floors Castle
Melrose
Lanark
Kelso
Lowick
DAY 1
Peebles
Biggar
DAY 3
Douglas
Wandylaw
Hawick
DAY 2
Jedburgh
Alnwick
Cramlington
Beattock
Northumberland National Park
Lochmaben
NEWCASTLE-UPON-TYME
ENGLAND

EXCURSION

THE SCOTTISH BORDERS

The Borders to the south of Scotland may still bear the scars of battles with neighboring England, but it is here that ruined abbeys, castles steeped in history, and rural villages can be found nestling among rolling hills and meandering rivers. There is also a flourishing textile industry that made the area the birthplace of tweed.

DAY 1: MELROSE

While not the best preserved of the four Cistercian abbeys in the region, Melrose undeniably possesses a unique poetic power. It was founded in the twelfth century, but although softened by time, its Gothic arches, gargoyles, and pink stone have survived to this day. Legend has it that the heart of Robert the Bruce (1274–1329), king of Scotland, lies buried here, lending the abbey a mystical aura. A short stroll away are the sandstone houses, cafés, and floral gardens of the village, where the Mainstreet Trading Company, a café-deli-bookshop is a favorite haunt of locals and tourists alike.

DAY 2: HAWICK

Hawick, further to the south, is the embodiment of manufacturing in the Borders. The Borders Textile Towerhouse museum, housed in a restored sixteenth-century building, chronicles the history of the tweed and knitted textiles that made the region's name. Just around the corner, a distillery has been set up in the town's old power station. The Borders Distillery is upholding tradition with a Scottish single malt whisky and breaking new ground with its gin and vodka.

DAY 3: JEDBURGH AND KELSO

Continue east to the village of Jedburgh and its majestic abbey. The nave, which is now open to the elements, slender columns, and quiet cloisters are a reminder of both the grandeur of the building and past conflicts. Kelso is situated further north, at the confluence of the Tweed and the Teviot. Kelso's great town square, a former market place, is cobbled and one of the largest in Scotland. Built in 1803 and used as a model for Waterloo Bridge in London, the five-arches of Kelso Bridge span the River Tweed. Floors Castle, the largest inhabited home in the country, lies on the outskirts of the town. Its turrets, lavishly decorated rooms, and beautiful gardens were built at the turn of the eighteenth century in the middle of a vast estate.

DAY 4: ST ABB'S HEAD AND THE COAST

To the north east, the Scottish Borders open out onto the North Sea, where the coastline becomes wilder and more rugged, in particular at St Abb's Head, a windswept promontory of steep cliffs and heather moors plunging down into the sea. Flocks of seabirds congregate in the National Nature Reserve here, and the shifting light lends the scenery a rare intensity. The village of St Abbs is a picturesque small port where visitors can stroll among fishing boats and limewashed cottages.

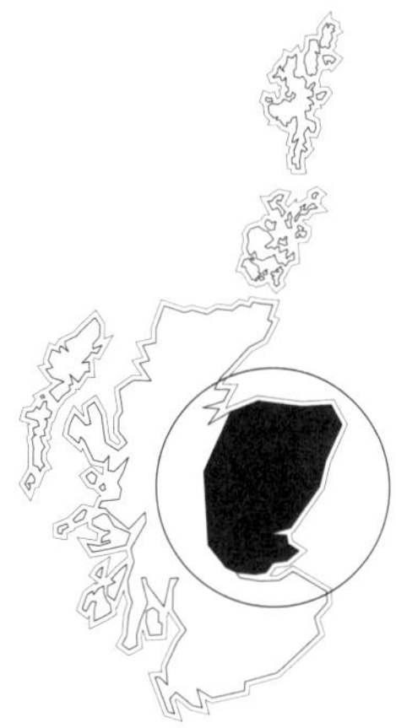

BETWEEN LAND AND SEA

CENTRAL SCOTLAND

From the rugged coastland of Aberdeenshire to the foothills of the Southern Highlands, taking in the green uplands of Perthshire and the Fife Peninsula, the central part Scotland contains a wide range of striking landscapes.

P.38

Ryvoan Bothy stands proudly among the heather of the Cairngorms National Park.

OPPOSITE

From Guardswell Farm, it's a short walk to the top of the hill where there is a rather unusual shelter.

The A9 is the major road that heads north from Perth to Inverness, with magnificent scenery almost from the very outset. The region of Perthshire, described by the writer Sir Walter Scott as "the fairest spot in the northern kingdom," is a heady blend of softly rounded hills, thousand-year-old forests, and Munros (peaks with an elevation of more than 3,000 ft/914 m). With its independent stores, cafés, and restaurants beside the River Tay, Dunkeld is one of the most attractive towns in the area. Traveling north from Perth, the first wave of Scottish castles begins to appear, the very first being the impressive Georgian manor house of Scone Palace, followed by Blair Castle, which seems to have landed straight out of a fairytale.

Castles are part of the very soul of the country, with the Grampians region to the northeast having its fair share—almost seventy are scattered around the region, including Balmoral, the royal family's Scottish residence situated between the villages of Braemar (birthplace of the Highland Games) and Ballater. Follow the course of the River Dee to find the wild and broad valley scenery of Royal Deeside that so charmed Queen Victoria. It eventually winds its way east to Aberdeen, the granite capital of Aberdeenshire and the departure points for ferries to the islands of Orkney and Shetland.

Before arriving in Speyside, a region to the west of Aberdeen that on its own contains nearly half the distilleries in the entire country and even has its own Malt Whisky Trail, be sure to stop off in the majestic Cairngorms National Park. This was created by the Scottish Parliament in 2003 as the largest of its kind in Scotland, extending over more than 1,745 square miles (4,500 km^2). This wild landscape of rugged beauty, with its moorland, lochs, and heaths, also includes Ben Macdui, Scotland's second-highest peak at 4,295 ft (1,309 m) and home to the only wild reindeer in Great Britain, thanks to Mikel Utsi, a Sámi from Sweden, who reintroduced a herd of reindeer here in 1952.

Travelers will therefore already have had a taste of the Highlands, with just a hint of the wealth of scenery that awaits them further north. Eastern central Scotland is less rugged than the Northern Highlands, but is every bit as beautiful as the rest of the country. From the jagged cliffs of the North Sea coast to the peaks of the Cairngorms, the region offers a playground for the wildest stretches of the imagination.

THE ESSENTIALS

13

KENMORE

Hike up to Black Rock Viewpoint for a fabulous vantage point overlooking Loch Tay and the village of Kenmore.

14

ST ANDREWS

St Andrews may have been where Scotland's first university was founded, but the town is now famous for its golf courses.

15

BLAIR CASTLE

The ancestral seat of the dukes of Atholl is worth a visit for its gardens and Victorian ballroom decorated with a mere one hundred and seventy-five sets of stag antlers.

16

BALMORAL CASTLE

Here, in the heart of the Cairngorms National Park, is the favorite residence of the British royal family, a gift from Prince Albert to his wife Queen Victoria in 1852.

17

CAIRNGORMS NATIONAL PARK

The largest national park in the United Kingdom has an area of 1,748 square miles (4,528 km^2) and boasts craggy peaks, lochs, rivers, and immense forests.

18

DUNKELD

Look out for the impressive cathedral and a host of cafés and stores in this charming small town on the banks of the River Tay.

19

DUNNOTTAR CASTLE

Perched high up overlooking the North Sea, this is one of the most spectacular ruins you could hope to see.

ABOVE

Travelers can stay the night in the Larch Cabin, tucked away in a valley in the Ochil Hills.

OPPOSITE

The cabin lies on the historic path that runs along the Arndean Valley from the village of Dollar to Rumbling Bridge.

EXPERIENCE

GUARDSWELL FARM

OPEN-AIR LIVING

From its vantage point on the brow of a hill overlooking the Tay, the longest river in Scotland, Guardswell Farm is reinventing farm life by offering people a place for meeting and sharing. This is where agriculture meets gastronomy and hospitality, intertwined with craftsmanship and wellness in a variety of activities in an atmosphere that is both joyful and tranquil, just as its founders intended.

There are some places where you can feel the winds of freedom blowing, and this is certainly the case in this small corner of Perthshire an hour and half's drive from Edinburgh. The Lamotte family took ownership of Guardswell, a 180-acre (approximately 72-hectare) hillside estate in 2011. In their desire to take care of the property to the best of their ability, Anna and her husband Digby envisioned a farm that respects all living things, not merely by preserving what already existed but also by striving to regenerate it. To achieve this, the couple have been increasing the diversity of flora, fauna, and funghi alike, reducing their carbon footprint, preserving living and fertile soil, and in general, creating a resilient farm that respects animal welfare and feeds the local community. Their farm and its kitchen garden are therefore surrounded by pastureland, woods, ponds, and marshes.

With her sunny personality and infectious good humor, Anna tells tales of her grandfather's dairy and herb farm, her great-grandmother's milk bar, and the garden café run by her parents to explain her professional path to date. Although she had once considered training as a chef, she eventually chose a career as farmer/entrepreneur, adding her own unique twist—life on the estate is punctuated with weddings, workshops (yoga, woodcarving, felted wool mat-weaving, cheese making, and more), dinner parties, and gatherings. There are six cabins where visitors can stay overnight on site, from a shepherd's hut to a modern country cottage on top of the hill.

The days here revolve around tending the organic kitchen garden, looking after the animals, and brewing cider from local apples and wild yeasts. Each livestock breed has been selected with great care, from the angora goats with their splendid curly fleeces (which yield excellent mohair), to the Hebrides sheep, a native breed that are perfect for keeping down the wildflower meadow and are also prized for their wool and meat. These mingle freely with a small herd of Shetland cattle, a rare and hardy breed that has adapted perfectly to the Scottish environment.

By inviting curious visitors to come and stay at Guardswell, Anna and Digby hope to encourage them to reconnect with a life that is simple and joyful, in harmony with the seasons and respectful of the living world. The couple also hope to pass on the principles of adopting a diet that is more closely linked to our surroundings and roots.

RECONNECTING

Visitors to Guardswell Farm can explore the farm at their own pace and spend more time with nature.

NOURISHING

Anna is carrying on her family's traditions in her own way, with the help of her husband Digby.

Sundown at Guardswell Farm, sheltered by the Perthshire hills.

ABOVE

The post office in the small village of Strathtay, on the banks of the River Tay.

OPPOSITE

Local people enjoying a summer dip in the Tay,
the longest river in the country.

ABOVE

The village of Kenmore lies on the banks of Loch Tay, where sailboats and paddleboards can often be seen in action.

OPPOSITE

An encounter with a ram during a hike in Glen Tilt.

NATURE

CAIRNGORMS NATIONAL PARK

SCOTTISH MOORLAND

The Cairngorms is the largest national park in the United Kingdom, encompassing high plateaus, mountain ranges, and vast pine forests within one of the most extensive and well-preserved natural areas in Scotland.

WHITE CROFT COMPANY

A small family-run business set in a traditional croft near Loch an Eilein.

UNDULATING HILLSIDES

Summer mountains covered in heather.

GLEN TILT

Dense forest in the south of the national park leads to Glen Tilt.

CAIRNGORM REINDEER HERD

A herd of reindeer has been living on 10 acres (4 ha) of mountainside since 1952.

LOCH ALVIE

The B9152 road that skirts the national park makes its way through pastureland and forests in turn as it runs along the shores of Loch Alvie.

AN LOCHAN UAINE

A beautiful loch with turquoise water and a sandy beach.

GLENMORE FOREST PARK

A landscape where bare mountains give way to thick forest.

NATURE RESTORED

Visitors to the park can meet the only wild reindeer in Great Britain here.

The Invereshie and Inshriach National Nature Reserve on the edge of the Cairngorms Plateau consists of pine forests and heathland.

Coming across a herd of newly shorn sheep on the way to the Invereshie and Inshriach National Nature Reserve.

ABOVE

A Highland cow in a meadow in the village of Blair Atholl, which is famous for its castle.

OPPOSITE

The fortified gates of the village of Blair Atholl, near the River Tilt. The village has been constructed using gray stone that is quarried locally.

Max Speed 20

TRADITION

THE HIGHLAND GAMES

THE SOUL OF SCOTLAND

The sound of the bagpipes, the tug-of-war, tossing the caber, livestock shows ... From the Orkneys to the Scottish borders, the Highland Games have a long history and are still attracting the crowds, being deeply rooted in Scotland's cultural history.

At the end of August, the excitement in the small town of Aberfeldy is palpable as a parade of pipers leads curious spectators from the center of town to the rugby club pitch beyond Wade's Bridge, which gracefully spans the Tay. No one is interested in rugby today, however. The Highland Games are held here every year, with similar events staged in thirty or so other towns and villages across Scotland. Events include a pony show, tug-of-war, a vintage tractor parade, and ceilidh dancing.

While no one is quite sure of the origins of the games, many historians agree that they first originated not far from Aberfeldy in Aberdeenshire. King Malcolm III, who ruled in the eleventh century, is said to have decided to organize a running race to the summit of Creag Chòinnich near Braemar to find the fastest runners in the country (who would then become his personal messengers), and hill racing remains one of the most popular events to this day.

Although the games have evolved considerably over the centuries, the modern version dates back to the end of the eighteenth century, after the Jacobite Rising of 1745 had made it all the more essential to preserve Scottish culture. The Falkirk games of 1781 included athletic feats, bagpipe playing, dancing, and tests of strength. By the turn of the nineteenth century, similar games were being held throughout the country and would sometimes include horse racing, individual bagpiping competitions, and even haggis hurling. They were held in Braemar for the first time in 1817 and would go on to become the most prestigious games in the country. Queen Victoria was a guest in 1848 and it was not uncommon to see members of the royal family in attendance.

The creation of the Scottish Games Association (SGA) in 1946 formalized the games and established rules, kept records, and introduced anti-doping testing. Some two hundred games were held in Scotland in the 1940s. The number has since declined, with twenty-eight events officially recorded in 2025, but they are nonetheless essential events in the Scottish cultural calendar. The season opens each May with the Gourock Highland Games and lasts until mid-September.

AN UNMISSABLE EVENT

The Highland Games season comes to a peak during the summer months.

POPULAR GAMES

The caber toss, tug-of-war, hammer-throwing, Highland dancing, and music are all part of the Highland Games.

ABOVE

Tractor parades are often a feature of these events, as are shows of Scottish livestock breeds.

OPPOSITE

The Highland Games are an important date in the calendar for many Scots.

AberfeldyShowAndGames.co.uk
2nd WEEKEND IN AUGUST

DEEP DIVE

TARTAN

Tartan is far more than just a fabric—it has become a timeless emblem of Scotland. This woven pattern of interlocking bands of color embodies the identity and memory of an entire people and now exists in several thousands of variations.

According to the official definition in the Scottish Register of Tartans Act (2008), tartan is "a design which is capable of being woven, consisting of two or more alternating colored stripes which combine vertically and horizontally to form a repeated chequered pattern," and "a tartan pattern is traditionally known as a 'sett' of tartan."

Although tartan-like cloth has been recorded in Scotland since the third century, it was primarily worn by the clans of northern Scotland (the Highlanders) during the seventeenth and eighteenth centuries. This tough, durable fabric is traditionally made from wool colored with dye made from local plants (such as ferns and lichens), whose shades of red, blue, and green recall the landscapes in which they grow.

The mid-eighteenth century saw tartan become a symbol of allegiance to Charles Edward Stuart, better known as Bonnie Prince Charlie. In 1745 the prince, who had been raised a Catholic, led a Jacobite rebellion seeking to topple the Protestant King George II and restore the Stuart dynasty, whose origins lay in Scotland. His supporters wore tartan but, after a resounding defeat at the Battle of Culloden the following year, the wearing of tartan was banned. Highlanders were then obliged to adopt the more close fitting, European-style clothing of the Lowlands (South and Southeast Scotland).

In 1782 the wearing of tartan became legal again and by the first decades of the nineteenth century followers of the Romantic movement had also begun to adopt it. In 1822 King George IV even appeared in traditional Highland dress during the first visit by an English monarch to Scotland since the Battle of Culloden. Twenty years later, it was Queen Victoria who took to wearing tartan with great enthusiasm. She played a part in the design becoming a real Scottish icon, evolving from a symbol of clan membership to a genuine fashion statement. This Scottish pattern is now a part of contemporary fashion history too, from Vivienne Westwood, who dressed the Sex Pistols in the 1970s, to Alexander McQueen, who made use of clan MacQueen tartan in 1995.

In 2008 the Scottish Parliament created the Scottish Register of Tartans, an independent and unique document that tracks and records the history of tartan. Hundreds of new patterns are registered every year, bringing their number to over seven thousand, with each extending the thread of an ever-evolving story.

TRADITIONAL DRESS AND TARTAN

1 / FOLK DRESS

Traditional Scottish dress follows a strict dress code based around the kilt. Pockets are replaced by a sporran, the short Argyll jacket flatters the figure, and the half-hose socks and long-laced shoes are ideally adapted for the climatic conditions and terrain of the Highlands.

VARIANT 1
Clan Campbell (base)

VARIANT 2
Clan Campbell of Breadalbane

VARIANT 3
Clan Campbell of Cawdor

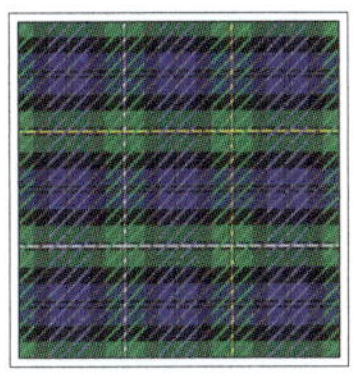

VARIANT 4
Clan Campbell of Loudoun

2 / THE EVOLUTION OF TARTAN WITHIN THE SAME CLAN

The great Scottish clans gradually separated out into different factions over time, each adopting variations of the same tartan. These variants all share a common base while introducing new colors or proportions that permit precise identification of familial or territorial allegiance.

ABOVE

West Sands Beach to the north of St Andrews stretches for almost two miles (3 km), surrounded by dunes and world-renowned golf courses.

OPPOSITE

Locals taking a dip at the foot of the castle in St Andrews, the town in which Scotland's first university was founded.

Grey Cairns of Camster
Lossiemouth
Elgin
Keith
Turriff
Peterhead
Inverness
Huntly
Inverurie
Alford
Aberdeen
DAY 4
Milton of Crathes
Balmoral Castle
Tarmachan Cafe
Ballater
DAY 3
The Fife Arms
DAY 2
The Highlanders Bakehouse
Bridge of Dye
Stonehaven
Cairngorms National Park
Braemar
DAY 1
Glensaugh
Dunnottar Castle
Killiecrankie
Kirriemuir
Blairgowrie and Rattray
Birnam
Arbroath
DUNDEE
NORTH SEA
Perth
St Andrews
Auchtermuchty
Auchterarder

EXCURSION

ABERDEENSHIRE

From the wild uplands of the Cairngorms National Park to the granite city of Aberdeen and its scenic coastline, not to mention the illustrious royal residence of Balmoral, a tour through Aberdeenshire promises many delights, including castles, picturesque villages, dense forests, and jagged peaks.

DAY 1: BRAEMAR AND THE CAIRNGORMS NATIONAL PARK

The village of Braemar, now famous for the Highland Games that are regularly attended by the British royal family, is a charming base from which to begin exploration of the Aberdeenshire region. If unable to attend the event (held at the beginning of September) in person, a trip to the Braemar Highland Games Centre is highly recommended before settling in at the Fife Arms, a renowned local institution in the heart of the Cairngorms National Park. This is the perfect starting point for exploring this wild region of rolling hills.

DAY 2: BALLATER AND BALMORAL CASTLE

Balmoral Castle has been the Scottish residence of the British Crown for more than a century, since the day in 1852 that Prince Albert gifted the estate to his wife Queen Victoria. Construction of the fairytale manor house began in 1853 and it is now surrounded by magnificent gardens (of particular interest to King Charles III) and nearly 50,000 acres (20,000 ha) of moors, heathland, hills, and forests. You can even spend the night in one of the thirteen cottages on the estate. Take the road into the center of the village of Ballater and be sure to stop off at the Highlanders Bakehouse artisan bakery, unless you would rather try one of Tarmachan Café's famous venison sausage rolls?

DAY 3: THE ROYAL DEESIDE RAILWAY AND STONEHAVEN

One detour in particular is worth making before reaching the coast: visitors to Milton of Crathes can leap aboard the steam train that until 1966 was used by the royal family to reach Balmoral Castle. The journey of about a mile (1.5 km) takes fifteen minutes or so and chugs its way through scenery once dear to Queen Victoria's heart. Afterwards, head to Stonehaven, a picturesque fishing village from whose harbor there's a path to the spectacular medieval ruins of Dunnottar Castle, on a headland overlooking the North Sea.

DAY 4: ABERDEEN

As you travel along the coast, Aberdeen eventually comes into view—a granite city with a character unique among the landscapes of Scotland that also boasts a vibrant cultural scene focused on art, fine dining, and festivals. The neoclassical architecture of Aberdeen Art Gallery houses one of the finest collections of paintings in the United Kingdom. The city's harbor is the departure point for ferries bound for Orkney and Shetland, a reminder that Aberdeen is still a major maritime hub.

FAR-FLUNG CORNERS

THE NORTHERN HIGHLANDS

A place where the imagination can run riot, a terrain in which isolation and ruggedness are part and parcel of the beauty of the scenery. This is a journey to the ends of the earth where, from the bays to the mountains, the traveler's only companions are likely to be Highland cattle, majestic stags, and seabirds.

P. 70

With their lochs, moorland, and mountains, the Northern Highlands offer glimpses of a Scotland that is rough and rugged, carved out by the elements.

OPPOSITE

A house with a garden full of flowers, not far from Loch Ness.

Inverness is the capital of the Highlands, the name deriving from the Scots Gaelic term *Inbhir Nis*, "the mouth of the Ness." This is the river that flows into the famous loch that forms part of the Great Glen, which in turn marks the boundary between the Northwest Highlands and the Grampian Mountains to the south. Inverness is therefore the gateway to the north and the starting point of the North Coast 500, a trail that extends for 500 miles (830 km) as it circumnavigates the northern tip of Scotland.

John O'Groats, far to the northeast, is one of the most northerly points in mainland Great Britain. According to one legend, at the end of the fifteenth century King James IV granted a Dutchman named Jan de Groot the right to operate a ferry from the coast to Orkney, which had recently become part of Scotland. The business became so successful that his seven children could not agree who should take it over. Disappointed at his offspring's squabbling, Jan resolved to build an octagonal house with eight doors, inside which an octagonal table would allow everyone to take an equal seat—no one would be at the head of the table. This way, at least, Jan got to eat his meals in peace. The modern ferry service now sails from Thurso to Orkney, a group of seventy islands with a wealth of archeological sites.

The northern coast is carved up into a series of cliffs, bays, and beaches of fine sand, with a host of small islands lying just offshore. To the east, the scenery becomes even more rugged heading toward the most beautiful landscapes of northeastern Sutherland and Assynt. The sense of isolation here is overwhelming, with just a handful of villages scattered along a coastline that has been left almost entirely to nature. The only way to reach these settlements is via the single-lane coast road with passing places to allow vehicles to squeeze by two abreast. The terrain further inland is a mixture of dark lochs, jagged mountains, and wild panoramas, dominated by Ben More (3,852 ft/1,174 m) and Ben Hope (3,041 ft/927 m).

If Inverness is the gateway to the eastern part of the Northern Highlands, Ullapool is the way into the west. This charming fishing port with its rows of white houses along the shores of Loch Broom is bustling with activity thanks to the ferry service to Lewis and Harris, which has opened the way to the Outer Hebrides.

THE ESSENTIALS

CLACHTOLL BEACH

This beach of white sand on the northwest coast of the Highlands is ringed by rock formations that provide at least some protection from the swell. The beach looks out over shallow waters and a landscape sculpted by erosion and Atlantic gales.

21

SMOO CAVE

This mysterious grotto in the historic county of Sutherland features a network of chambers carved out by marine and river erosion.

22

EAS A' CHUAL ALUINN WATERFALL

There's a great view of these falls, the highest in the United Kingdom (660 ft/200 m), from Loch Gleann Dubh.

23

ACHMELVICH BAY

A bay of light-colored sand surrounded by dunes and rocky outcrops that is a small detour from the coast road B869. It is known for the crystal clarity of its water.

24

LOCH NESS

This mysterious loch and its legend never fail to fire up the imagination.

25

ARDVRECK CASTLE

The ruins of Ardvreck Castle lie on the shores of Loch Assynt. These last remnants of an ancient Highland fortress still tower over the landscape.

26

DUNCANSBY STACKS

These dramatic rock pinnacles rising from the sea in the far northeastern corner of the North Coast 500 trail have been formed by erosion and offshore winds.

One hiking trail in the Loch Ness area leads to the Falls of Foyers and a vantage point with magnificent views over the surrounding countryside.

ABOVE

The Falls of Foyers consist of two waterfalls with a total drop of 140 ft (42 m). They flow into a winding gorge that eventually opens into Loch Ness.

OPPOSITE

A trip by kayak on the waters of Loch Ness.

NATURE

HIGHLAND CATTLE

THE ICONIC BREED OF THE HIGHLANDS

Instantly recognizable by their curved horns and straggly coats, Highland cows typify the picture postcard image of Scotland. Behind this photogenic animal, however, lies the long history of a breed that seems to have a promising future in the face of climate change.

Known to the Scots as the "Highland Coo," this is one of the oldest cattle breeds in the world. From its origins in the Highlands and Islands of the Outer Hebrides, it has learned to thrive and survive among harsh winters, poor soils, and biting winds. Its secret is a double-layered coat that is dense and wooly nearest the skin, and long and waterproof on top, allowing it to withstand the harshest conditions. There were originally two distinct types: the Kyloe, which was small and black and came from the islands, and the Highland, from the hinterlands of Scotland, which was larger and had a reddish-brown coat. The two strains gradually interbred to give rise to the version we know today.

Although Highland cattle are documented as far back as the sixth century, the breed was not officially recognized until 1885 when the first herd book was created by the Highland Cattle Society, which fixed its standards and registered its pedigrees. With its familiar long, silky coat and majestic horns, which point upward for females and forward or slightly downward for males, it has remained almost unchanged for centuries. Reddish-brown is still the most common color, but shades of yellow or blonde, gray, black, white, and a kind of yellowy-black can also be seen.

Highland cattle are no longer to be found exclusively in their Scottish homeland, but are now established all over the world, from Canada to Australia via France and Denmark. Their hardiness and ability to adapt to the most hostile environments, combined with the tender and uniquely flavored beef they yield, have made them ideal providers of high-quality and environmentally friendly food. They are able to thrive on poor or marshy pastureland by grazing on what other animals pass over (reeds, brambles, thistles, and young tree shoots), which helps to preserve biodiversity and maintain open landscapes. The Highland cow is both an icon and a guardian of Scottish moorland, a hardy breed that seems destined to roam around the heathland of Scotland for many years to come.

A UNIQUE DOUBLE COAT

Highland cattle have coats made up of two layers, the uppermost layer being long, coarse, and oily, allowing them to withstand the harsh climate of the Highlands.

LONGEVITY

Highland cattle have a long lifespan and can expect to live to around twenty years of age on average, with some even surviving to twenty-five.

ABOVE

The fringe falling over the eyes of Highland cattle is known as a dossan, which is Gaelic for a "cowlick."

OPPOSITE

The Assynt coast road cuts inland toward Loch Assynt.

ESCAPE

THE COAST ROAD B869

ASSYNT

The coast road B869 winds through Assynt, linking small isolated communities and providing a whole succession of panoramic views over lochs, ancient mountains, and a very rugged coastline.

HORIZONS

The scenery alternates between rocky peaks and beaches surrounded by sand dunes.

PANORAMA

An island surrounded by the waters of Loch a' Chàirn Bhàin.

DRUMBEG

There is a lovely view of the beach and little islands from the village of Drumbeg.

COMMUNITY

The population of Assynt numbers around one thousand.

SHEEP FARMING

If there's any doubt that spring is here, just look at the lambs.

TAKING A STROLL

The road winds through the hills as it cuts inland from the coast.

CROFTER

An abandoned house looks out over the village of Drumbeg.

LOCHS

The road skirts loch after loch as it moves inland.

ABOVE

Eddrachilles Hotel on the Northwest Highland coast is the perfect place to stop off while traveling the North Coast 500.

OPPOSITE

The hotel gardens look out over Badcall Bay and are filled with all kinds of indigenous wild flowers.

Loch Assynt is around 6 miles (10 km) long and surrounded by windswept hills.

DEEP DIVE

THE CLANS OF SCOTLAND

Clan membership is emblematic of the way Scottish society is organized, with the clans symbolizing both a deep connection to the land and a certain spirit of rebellion. Clan tartans are officially recorded and registered by the Scottish Register of Tartans, a role previously performed by the Lord Lyon King of Arms, and remain a source of great pride that continue to fire the imagination.

The word "clan" (which is derived from Scots Gaelic *clann*, "children") originally referred to a family with a father at its head. This patriarch would then be succeeded by his son, explaining the introduction of prefix "Mac-" (meaning "son of") before a surname. By extension, a clan designates a group of people united by a shared family name, whether related by blood or choice. This name is closely associated with the land where the group lives.

The way a clan was organized was inherited from Celtic society and revolved around a chief who was actively engaged in defending a territory. Each clan has its own motto (in English, Gaelic, Latin, or sometimes even in French) and its own tartan. From the thirteenth century onward, these mini-societies lived off the land and raised cattle from their bases in the Highlands. These farming activities gave rise to many rivalries that were compounded by border conflicts often settled with bloodshed.

The Scottish clan system was at its height just before the Battle of Culloden in 1746, when the Jacobite Rebellion was brought to an end by King George II's royalist forces led by the Duke of Cumberland. The clans suffered devastating losses, with around one thousand five hundred of Scotland's clansmen dying on the field.

Traditional Highland dress was subsequently outlawed under the Dress Act (which was repealed only in 1782) and the land belonging to Bonnie Prince Charlie's supporters was confiscated by the Crown. From around 1750 Highlanders were thrown out of their homes and clan members were obliged to resettle in small tenant farms, the start of a period known as the Highland Clearances. The resulting overpopulation and competition for land meant that many had no choice but to seek new horizons and emigrate.

After a century of decline and repression, interest in the clans was revived with the advent of Romanticism in the nineteenth century. The author Sir Walter Scott was a leading light in this movement and even orchestrated King George IV's visit to Scotland in 1822 with a view to promoting Highland tradition with tartan pageantry and clan identity. A fascination with genealogy and heritage played a similar role in the rebirth of clan identity during the reign of Queen Victoria. Clan affiliation continues to fire the imagination to this day, as the many museums, gatherings, and Highland Games will testify, reminding us that the spirit of Robert the Bruce and the Macpherson and Murray clans still watches over Scotland.

THE CLANS

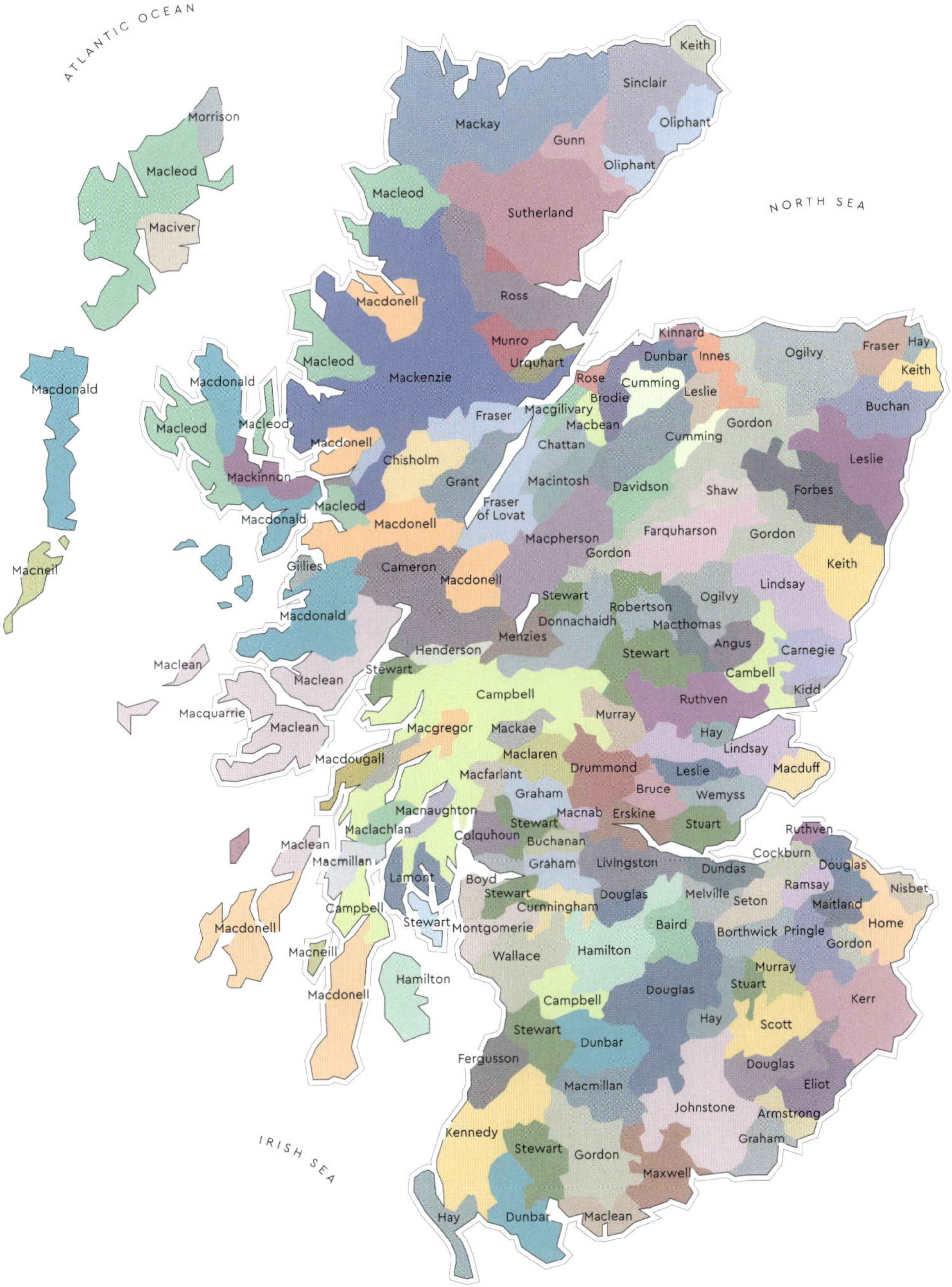

TERRITORIES AND LINEAGES

Scottish clan structure is strongly based on territorial roots, with each clan historically being associated with a particular region. The clans were constructed around ties of kinship, control of land, and local alliances, and so shaped the social and political organization of the country.

ABOVE

Once one of the most densely populated areas in the country, the Sutherland region is now sparsely inhabited, but is still a prime destination for anglers.

OPPOSITE

There's a good chance of spotting a seal near the fishing hamlet of Kylesku.

EXPERIENCE

SCOTLAND BY TRAIN

Many a traveler has dreamed of touring Scotland by train, and the country has a long tradition of travel by railroad that began at the turn of the nineteenth century when lines of rail track began to snake their way through the countryside.

Railroad travel arrived in Scotland more than two hundred years ago when the first horse-drawn rail line was opened in 1808. While the first services mostly transported goods relating to industry, such as coal and other raw materials, the advent of steam power gradually opened up the train network to passengers. The Edinburgh–Glasgow line was inaugurated in 1842, the first link in a network that now crisscrosses the country, making it possible to explore otherwise inaccessible regions.

This is certainly the case with the West Highland Line, which has to be one of the most scenic lines in the world. It was completed in 1901 to connect Glasgow with Oban and Mallaig on the west coast, calling at Fort William and crossing the famous Glenfinnan Viaduct. Corrour railway station is the highest mainline station in the United Kingdom and accessible only by rail (or a twenty-mile walk). Situated among the vast peaks of the Grampian Mountains, it houses a restaurant (Corrour Station House) and several bed and breakfast rooms.

The line is used by famous trains such as the Jacobite Steam Train (whose steam locomotive crossing the Glenfinnan Viaduct has become legendary for fans of Harry Potter and many others) and the luxurious Belmond Royal Scotsman with its art deco railcars, which could well be the Scottish equivalent of the Orient Express.

Other less well-known lines are also worthy of exploration, such as the Kyle of Lochalsh Line in the Northern Highlands. It crosses the country from Dingwall, near Inverness in the east, to the Kyle of Lochalsh, a village in the west at the foot of the Isle of Skye, navigating a landscape of deep lochs, rugged mountains, and moorland as it does so. The Far North Line connecting Inverness and Thurso via Wick is the northernmost service in the United Kingdom, promising a picturesque journey along the North Sea coast that feels as though it is taking you to the ends of the earth. In Thurso continue your adventure by taking a ferry bound for the islands of Orkney or Shetland.

It sems as though trains are inseparable from a certain image of the Scottish landscape. In opening up access to the most remote areas, they are both a link between different worlds and a call to adventure.

AT THE ENDS OF THE EARTH

Thurso Station, which lies 335 miles (539 km) from Edinburgh, is the northernmost stop on the Far North Line and the northernmost extremity of the United Kingdom's rail network.

FACTS AND FIGURES

Scotland has nearly 2,668 miles (4,294 km) of railroad lines serving three hundred and sixty-two stations, connecting the major cities with the country's most remote regions.

Nature reigns supreme in Scotland. There are estimated to be around a million stags here in the wild.

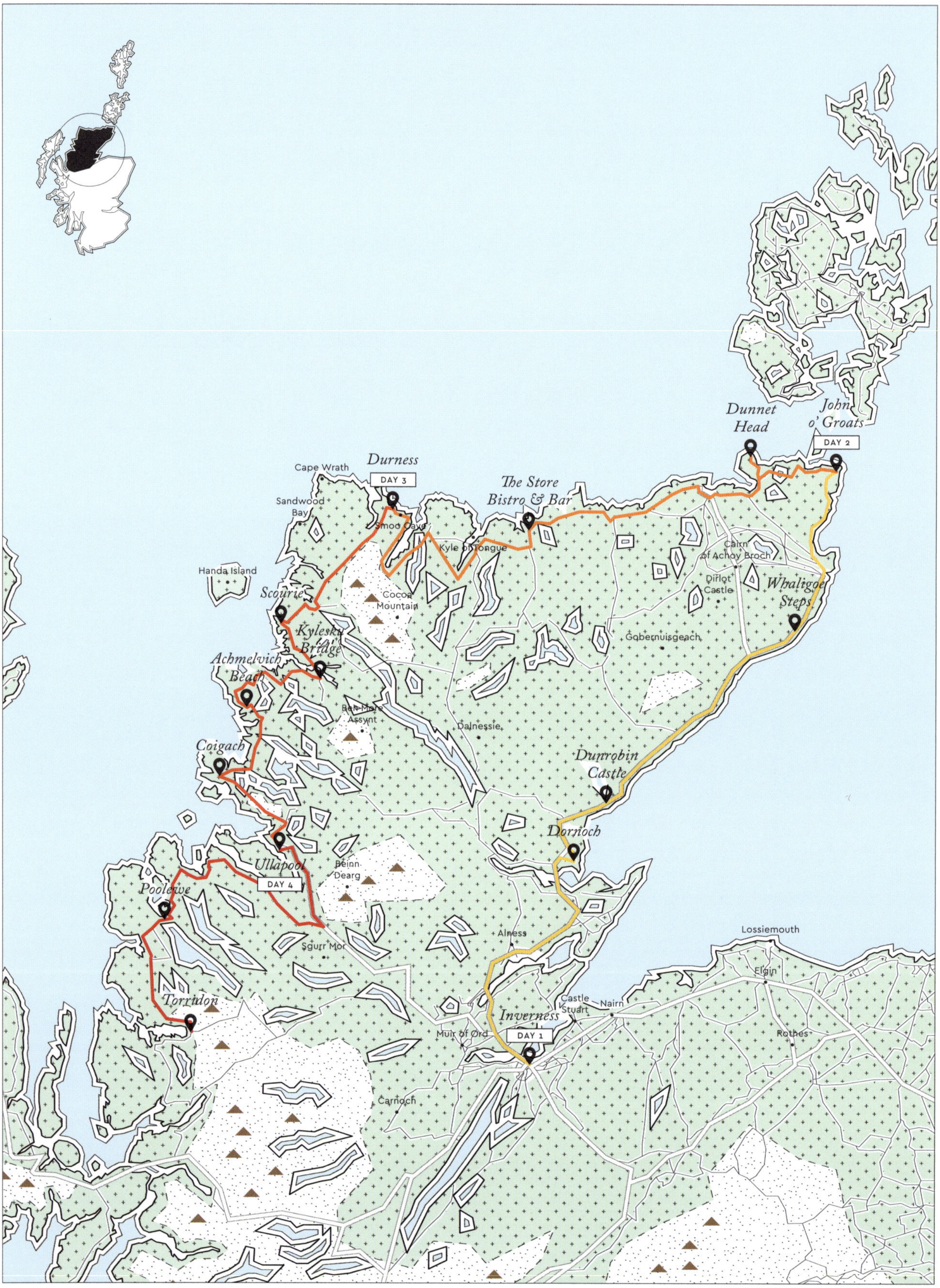

Cape Wrath
Durness
DAY 3
Sandwood Bay
Smoo Cave
The Store Bistro & Bar
Kyle of Tongue
Dunnet Head
John o' Groats
DAY 2
Cairn of Achoy Broch
Dirlot Castle
Whaligoe Steps
Gobernuisgeach
Handa Island
Scourie
Cocoa Mountain
Kylesku Bridge
Achmelvich Beach
Ben More Assynt
Dalnessie
Coigach
Dunrobin Castle
Dornoch
Ullapool
DAY 4
Beinn Dearg
Poolewe
Alness
Sgurr Mor
Lossiemouth
Elgin
Torridon
Castle Stuart
Nairn
Inverness
Muir of Ord
DAY 1
Rothes
Carnoch

EXCURSION

THE NORTH COAST 500

The North Coast 500 is a 516-mile (830-km) driving route around the Northern Highlands that has been nicknamed the Scottish Route 66. Starting from Inverness, it passes tranquil lochs and tall mountains as it follows the coastline past windswept cliffs and pristine beaches.

DAY 1: FROM INVERNESS TO JOHN O'GROATS

Shortly after Inverness the road hits the North Sea coast and once past Dornoch, a village with one of the oldest golf courses in the world, the fairytale turrets of Dunrobin Castle soon come into view. Continue to the vertiginous Whaligoe Steps, where the three hundred and thirty steps carved into the cliff were once used by fisherwomen carrying baskets of fish to the clifftop. This section of the route ends at John O'Groats in the far northeast of Scotland, but the most beautiful views are to be had a little further on at Duncansby Head, with its jutting cliffs of red sandstone and nesting colonies of seabirds. The Duncansby Stacks are a short walk from here.

DAY 2: FROM JOHN O'GROATS TO DURNESS

From John O'Groats the road leads to Dunnet Head, a remote peninsula where cliffs teeming with puffins create a striking backdrop. After a stop at The Store Bistro & Bar, the panorama opens up with a view across the Kyle of Tongue, a narrow sea loch overlooked by the mountains of Ben Loyal and Ben Hope. The spectacular Smoo Cave and the sand dunes of Balnakeil Beach near Durness herald a stop at Cocoa Mountain, an artisan chocolatier, store, and café.

DAY 3: FROM DURNESS TO ULLAPOOL

From Durness, the wild beach at Sandwood Bay points the way to Scotland's northwestern tip, watched over by the lighthouse at Cape Wrath. Take a boat from Scourie to Handa Island, a wildlife reserve with nesting puffins and guillemots, before calling in at the Shorehouse restaurant to try the locally caught crayfish. Kylesku Bridge spans a series of lochs just around the corner from the highest waterfalls in the country; the road then carries on to the turquoise waters and beach of Achmelvich Bay. The twists and turns of the single-track B869 lead to the magnificent Coigach Peninsula. The mountains of Assynt, dominated by the peak of Suilven, announce imminent arrival in Ullapool, a lively small port and the departure point for ferries to the Outer Hebrides.

DAY 4: FROM ULLAPOOL TO TORRIDON

Leaving Ullapool, the road skirts a series of lochs and mountains that offer beautiful scenery. The Inverewe Gardens in Poolewe benefit from a climate tempered by the Gulf Stream; their lush foliage is in striking contrast to the ruggedness of the surrounding mountains. A little further on, the mysterious Coille na Glas Letire ("wood of the grey slope"), an ancient forest of Caledonian pines carpeted in moss and lichen, leads to the Aird Mhòr Peninsula, a wild promontory looking out across the sea. Finally, the dramatic Torridon Hills come into view, with giant peaks of sandstone and quartzite.

NATURE AND ARCHEOLOGY

LEWIS AND HARRIS

Lewis and Harris is the northernmost island in the Outer Hebrides, whose breathtaking scenery is bound up with a deeply rooted Gaelic culture.

P. 100

Harris, to the south, has the most beautiful beaches on the island.

OPPOSITE

Crossing the empty landscape of North Harris, the horizon seems endless—but you never know who you might bump into.

An island with two names—this is the first thing that strikes the visitor to Lewis and Harris. Often overlooked by travelers, Lewis, to the north, consists of miles of moorland and windswept marshes without a single tree. Nevertheless, this is where Stornoway is located, the most populated town in the Outer Hebrides (which also include the islands of North Uist, Benbecula, South Uist, and Barra). It is a hub of Scots Gaelic culture, a language that is still spoken daily by nearly half the inhabitants, and since 2020 it has become the default teaching language in many schools. Religion and tradition still play a central role in the lives of islanders (who almost without exception attend the local Presbyterian churches) to the extent that many cafés, restaurants, and stores are closed on Sundays.

Harris, to the south, consists mainly of a rocky peninsula with a wild and jagged coastline punctuated by spectacular beaches of fine sand and turquoise waters. The Clan MacLeod (which also has a presence on the Isle of Skye) ruled the roost here for centuries, taking arms against the MacDonalds for control of the Hebrides. The word Hebrides is thought to derive from Old Norse meaning "the islands at the edge of the sea."

The island was first settled by groups of hunter-gatherers in around 8500 BCE and its rich history has been preserved to the present day through the many archeological sites that lie scattered across the landscape. The Calanais Standing Stones on the west coast of Lewis date back to the Neolithic period, while the Picts left behind *brochs*, circular towers of stone. Next it was the turn of the Vikings, who left their mark on the island until Norway ceded the Hebrides to Scotland in the 1266 Treaty of Perth.

Isolated by its geography, Lewis and Harris has had to demonstrate resilience over the centuries, but has equally been able to preserve strong local traditions. The globalization of the textile industry therefore failed to disrupt the island's economy, which has not only managed to preserve its Harris Tweed—the only fabric in the world to be protected by an Act of Parliament—but continues to manufacture it to this day.

THE ESSENTIALS

27

THE GOLDEN ROAD

This secluded road on the southeastern coast of Harris makes its way through what is at times a lunar-like landscape, with some of the most striking scenery on the island.

28

BUTT OF LEWIS

David and Thomas Stevenson built this lighthouse at the far northern tip of the island in 1862.

29

MANGERSTA SEA STACKS

Majestic, windswept cliffs on the west coast of Lewis.

30

CALANAIS STANDING STONES

This circle of stones is one of the largest megalithic sites in Scotland.

31

IRON HOUSE

Situated on the island of Great Bernera, this site dates back to the Iron Age.

32

GEARRANNAN BLACKHOUSE VILLAGE

A glimpse of crofter life in the nineteenth century.

33

STORNOWAY

Local services and institutions are based in Stornoway, the island's main town, including the Harris Tweed Authority, which is responsible for protecting and certifying the way traditional tweed is manufactured.

34

ST KILDA

Listed by UNESCO as a World Heritage Site, St Kilda is a group of islands that pushes the limits of adventure at what feels like the end of the world.

ABOVE

Sheep keeping an eye on things on the island of Great Bernera.

OPPOSITE

A beach of fine sand lies next to the reconstructed Bostadh Iron Age House.

ABOVE

Visitors can stay the night at Broad Bay House, a guesthouse just north of Stornoway on the east coast of Lewis.

OPPOSITE

The spacious sitting room offers fine views of the beach and the Atlantic Ocean.

ARTS AND CRAFTS

HARRIS TWEED

Harris Tweed is the only fabric in the world to be protected by law and owes its very survival to a hundred or so islanders who were determined to preserve a skill that had been passed down for generations.

Rebecca Hutton spends the majority of her time in a wooden shed behind her house. Her workshop is a cheerful riot of skeins of wool, color samples, and tools with the patina of age, with a large loom taking center stage. Working under the name Taobh Tuath Tweeds, this young woman is one of over one hundred and fifty active independent weavers endorsed by the Harris Tweed Authority, which certifies genuine Harris Tweed. This fabric made from pure virgin wool, known for its durability, is transformed into a rich tapestry of colors and textures beneath her hands.

Although this is a craft that has been practiced by the islanders of Lewis and Harris, Uist, and Barra for some two and a half thousand years, it did not really take off until the mid-nineteenth century. Lady Catherine Murray, Countess of Dunmore and widow of the Earl of Dunmore, the landowner of Harris, devoted herself to promoting tweed to her rich friends and it speedily caught on in London salons, finding its way onto the shelves of the United Kingdom's major retailers.

By the turn of the twentieth century, the tweed industry was in full swing, but the specter of counterfeit goods was looming. The Harris Tweed Association was founded in 1909 to register a trademarked logo consisting of an orb topped by a Maltese Cross with "Harris Tweed" written beneath—the Orb Certification Mark. The fabric's future was ultimately assured with the passing of the Harris Tweed Act 1993, which linked the fabric with the islands forever.

In order to bear the Harris Tweed name, each length of fabric must conform to precise criteria. According to law, the fabric must be made from one hundred percent pure virgin wool that has been dyed and spun in a mill on the islands of the Outer Hebrides, prior to being woven by hand in the home of an island weaver. There are three such mills still operating on Lewis and Harris.

Carloway Mill on the west coast of Lewis, is the oldest of these. Amid a cloud of smoke and steam, its machinery (which dates back to 1892) uses a special technique to dye the wool in which individual fabric dyes are mixed according to precise recipes. A single thread can contain several colors, perfectly recreating the colors of local heathland, lochs, and mountains. It is a poetic way of rooting the fabric within its scenic surroundings and providing a reminder of its origins.

PASSING IT ON

The Harris Tweed Story Room in Stornoway explains the fabric's history and highlights the role of the Harris Tweed Authority.

THE CRAFT

Rebecca Hutton is one of the independent weavers active on Lewis and Harris.

Most of the roads in the southern part of Harris are single-lane, so vehicles have to squeeze past each other at designated passing places.

Luskentyre on the west coast of Harris has one of the island's most beautiful beaches, where ponies freely wander the dunes.

ABOVE

The island's sheep provide the one hundred percent pure virgin wool required to manufacture Harris Tweed.

OPPOSITE

Tarbert is the departure point for ferries bound for the Isle of Skye and also marks the border between South and North Harris and Lewis.

DEEP DIVE

THE BOTHIES

Bothies are ancient shelters scattered throughout the remotest parts of Scotland. They have stood the test of time, preserving the philosophy of exploring the great outdoors in a way that is free and accessible to everyone.

The term bothy (or bothie) originates from the Scots Gaelic word *bothan*, meaning "hut." These remote rustic shelters were constructed during the mid- to late eighteenth century to accommodate farmers, shepherds, and forest workers employed by landowners. However, with the arrival of the Industrial Revolution and the promise of more lucrative work in city factories, many were abandoned, contributing to the depopulation of the countryside.

By the 1930s, with the rise of hiking as a pastime, bothies were being used by young men and women from the towns and cities who wanted to spend more time in nature. The owners would turn a blind eye to the practice and "bothying" as an activity was born.

In 1965 a small group of like-minded walking enthusiasts decided to found the Mountain Bothies Association (MBA), an organization with the aim of maintaining "simple shelters in a remote country for the use and benefit of all who love wild and lonely places." The MBA now has some three thousand eight hundred members, and of the over one hundred shelters it looks after, eighty-three are located in Scotland, twelve in England, and nine in Wales. Modern bothying is based on respect for the environment, for other guests, and for the land on which the bothies are located. Bothies cannot be reserved and are completely free of charge, which encourages social interaction, but generally have no electricity or running water. Every visitor must abide by the Bothy Code laid down by the MBA. This is based on common sense—treating the shelter and its users with respect, respecting the countryside (by not cutting down trees for heating, for example), and taking your trash with you when you leave.

In the era of the internet and social media, bothy culture seems to be under threat, at least according to its oldest advocates. However, once passed on by word of mouth, the locations of the shelters are now easily discoverable in just a few clicks, and the 2017 publication of *The Scottish Bothy Bible* guidebook also contributed to an increase in the number of users.

The spirit of the bothy movement is also inspiring new projects. The Bothy Project was created in 2011 with a vision of contemporary shelters where artists and writers can live and work in an immersive atmosphere within the Scottish landscape. These modern, self-contained, minimalist spaces (such as Sweeney's Bothy on the island of Eigg) uphold the same philosophy: solitude, a slow pace of life, and an intimate connection with the countryside—but with added comfort.

SCOTTISH VERNACULAR HOMES

CROFT HOUSE

A traditional small farm dwelling with lime-washed walls, a slate roof, and two chimneys.

BOTHY

A basic, single-room stone building with few windows or doors and a roof of slate or sheet metal, in a remote location.

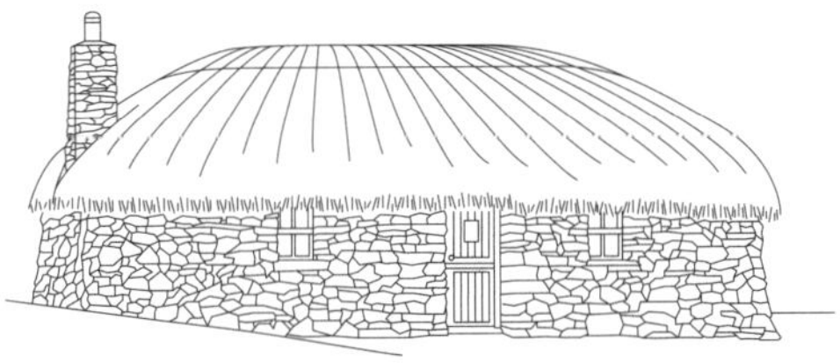

BLACKHOUSE

A squat dwelling with rounded corners and very thick walls made of stone and peat. The thatched roof is weighted down with stones and lashed in place, and the eaves overhang small apertures for windows and doors.

SHIELING

A seasonal shelter built of dry stone and peat on high-altitude pastureland, often close to a watercourse. They generally have few windows or none at all.

BUILDING WITH THE LANDSCAPE

Traditional forms of house building in Scotland are linked to the climate, local resources, and rural lifestyles. Whether permanent or seasonal, they use simple materials and are primarily designed to make the best use of the environment.

The hills of North Harris look out over beaches of white sand to the south.

TRADITIONAL SKILLS

CARLOWAY MILL

WEAVING

Carloway Mill on the Isle of Lewis is one of three weaving mills still in operation.

MATERIAL

Weavers work with one hundred percent pure virgin wool.

ARTS AND CRAFTS

The weavers make tweed by hand on a treadle loom.

A UNIQUE FABRIC

Harris Tweed is protected by an Act of Parliament.

PROCESSING

The wool is first washed and dyed before carding.

CERTIFICATION

Each batch is inspected by the Harris Tweed Authority before the famous orb logo is awarded and attached to the fabric as the final seal of approval.

WASTE NOT, WANT NOT

Nothing is thrown away, and fabric offcuts are turned into colored squares.

DYES

The dyed and white wools are woven according to strict patterns.

TECHNIQUE

The wool is carded by passing it through mechanical rollers with teeth that carefully untangle and align the fibers.

ABOVE

Several of the Royal Mail's instantly familiar red letterboxes are scattered across the island.

OPPOSITE

A single ray of sunlight is enough to light up the countryside on the coast road to South Harris.

ARCHEOLOGY

THE ISLAND TREASURES OF THE OUTER HEBRIDES

DIVE INTO HISTORY

Menhirs, Bronze Age chambered cairns, Iron Age fortifications ... Lewis and Harris is littered with archeological sites, with most formed from Lewisian gneiss, a metamorphic rock formed at the dawn of geological time.

No less than forty-seven stones, some far taller than a man, look out over Loch Roag on the west coast of Lewis. Arranged in the form of a Celtic cross around 405 ft (123 m) long with a central ring, they have been watching over the surrounding countryside for more than five millennia. The Calanais (Callanish, in English) Standing Stones were placed here between 2900 and 2600 BCE (probably earlier than the famous prehistoric stone circle at Stonehenge) and are one of the most important Neolithic sites in the country. Ranging in height from 3–16 ft (1–4.8 m), with the tallest being the central monolith, the stones were carved from Lewisian gneiss, a rock created by volcanic activity in the bowels of the Earth's crust more than three billion years ago.

Just a few miles down the road, travelers enter another era—Dun Carloway Broch is a circular tower built two thousand years ago, probably as a defensive structure, and is around 30 ft (9 m) tall. Its massive walls—anything up to 10 ft (3 m) thick—have many a tale to tell of the harshness of life here, sheltered behind its solid stone. The Bostadh settlement, a village dating back to the Iron Age, lies beside a beautiful bay with a beach of white sand on the nearby island of Great Bernera. It was exposed by a violent storm in 1993 and has since been entirely recovered with sand. A reconstruction has now been built on a nearby site, including a house with low ceilings and a thatched roof to protect inhabitants from the gales of the Atlantic. To continue this journey through time, visit the tiny village of Gearrannan, where nine late nineteenth-century blackhouses have been restored as the last group of such dwellings still in existence on the island. People were living here until the 1970s and the houses are a reminder of the everyday life of the crofters and farmers/fishermen who tended local smallholdings.

And finally, no discussion of the archeological heritage of the Outer Hebrides is complete without mentioning the island of South Uist, where two Bronze Age mummies were discovered at Cladh Hallan. It was a unique find that elevated the Outer Hebrides to a major archeological site on a par with Orkney. From the standing stones at Calanais to the Gearrannan blackhouses and the Uist mummies, these islands truly tell the story of five thousand years of Scottish history.

1 / GEARRANNAN BLACKHOUSE VILLAGE

This hamlet on the west coast of Lewis contains nine restored late nineteenth-century blackhouses.

2 / SEA VIEWS

The village is located right beside the Atlantic, from where it is a short walk to the top of the nearby cliffs.

3 / CALANAIS

Pause to give the imagination free rein at the Calanais Standing Stones formed of Lewisian gneiss.

4 / COUNTRY LIFE

The village is surrounded by mountains and pastureland.

5 / STAY

The blackhouses can be booked for an overnight stay.

ABOVE

Approximately 21,000 people live on Lewis and Harris.

OPPOSITE

Lobster pots awaiting use near the Bridge over the Atlantic, which links the island to Great Bernera.

RONA
SR79
RONA

Cattle grid

ABOVE

It is thought there are more than 8,000 wild stags on Lewis and Harris.

OPPOSITE

A road in Lewis winds its way between cattle pasture and rock.

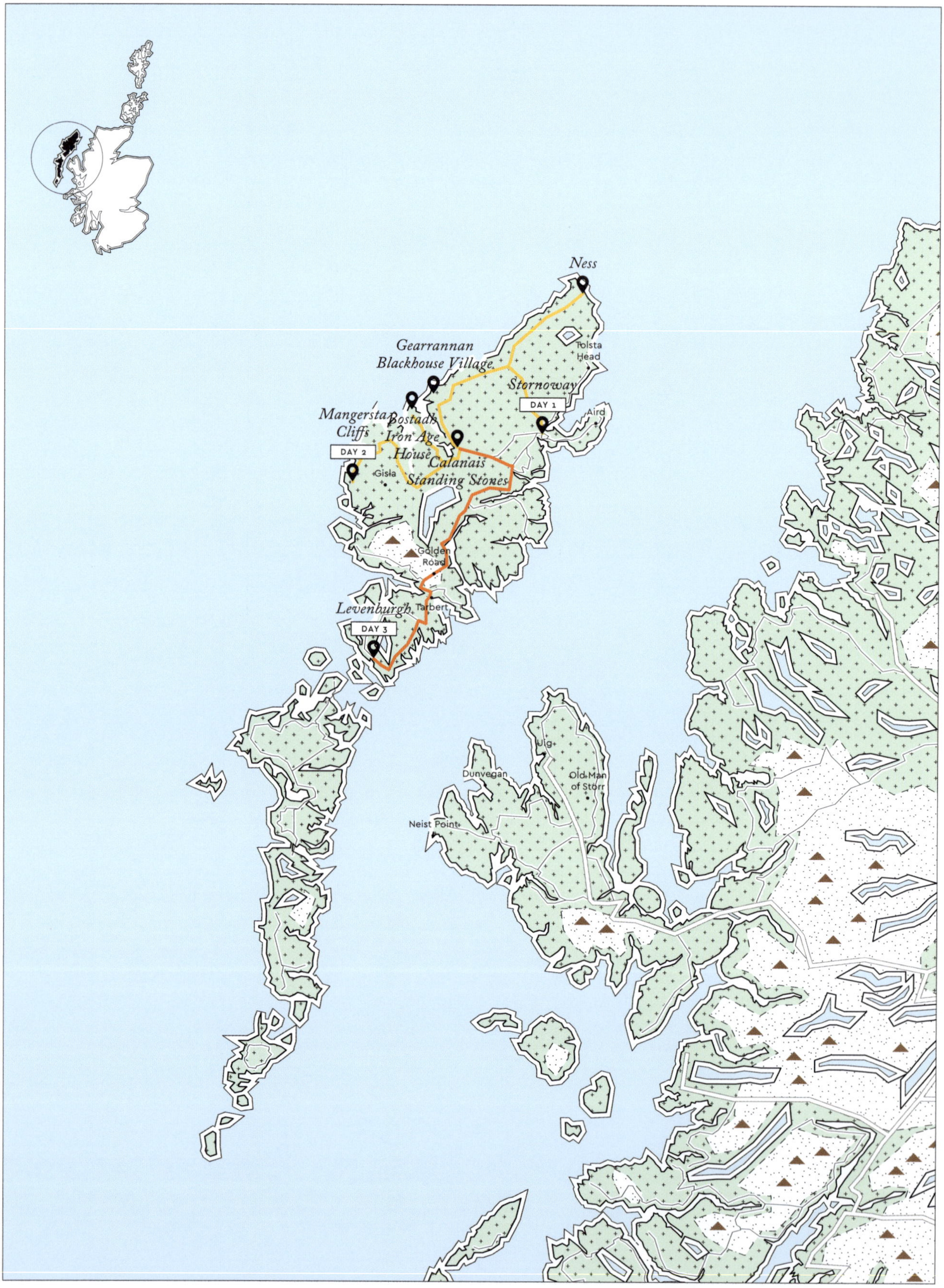
Ness
Tolsta Head
Gearrannan Blackhouse Village
Stornoway
DAY 1
Aird
Mangersta Cliffs
Bostadh Iron Age House
DAY 2
Calanais Standing Stones
Gisla
Golden Road
Levenburgh
Tarbert
DAY 3
Uig
Dunvegan
Old Man of Storr
Neist Point

EXCURSION

AN INSIDER'S TOUR OF LEWIS AND HARRIS

From cliffs battered by Atlantic gales to beaches of white sand, and from millennia-old megaliths to artisan workshops, Lewis and Harris represents a side of Scotland that has remained hidden. To cross the island from north to south is to explore a world where nature still reigns supreme.

DAY 1: THE EAST COAST OF LEWIS

Heading north from Stornoway, the road reaches the beach at Tràigh Mhòr, a ribbon of golden sand backed by dunes. You may be lucky enough to spot the silhouette of a minke whale or a basking shark from the promontory of Tolsta Head. Something unusual awaits travelers at the very end of the road—the Bridge to Nowhere is a crossing built in the 1920s for a road that was never finished. You will just have to turn round and head up the west coast to reach Ness. The port of Ness at the far northern tip of the island is where a line of colorful cottages cluster around a turquoise cove. People still speak Gaelic here and it is one of the last bastions of the language. The red-brick Butt of Lewis Lighthouse stands on a windswept headland overlooking the North Atlantic, where it feels as though you have reached the edge of the world. Turn south once again, and there is a wealth of archeological treasures to be discovered on the west coast: the circle of megaliths at Calanais, the blackhouses at Gearrannan, and Bostadh Iron Age Village. The less well-known site at Stac a' Phris contains a rocky, wave-battered arch that stands isolated above the turbulent water.

DAY 2: MANGERSTA AND UIG SANDS

Follow the road south to explore the dizzying backdrop of the Mangersta cliffs plunging down into the sea, rocky arches, and wave-battered sea stacks. The scenery here is in stark contrast with the beach at Ardroil (also known as Uig Sands), one of the most beautiful in Scotland, although this vast expanse of fine sand surrounded by dunes and hills is almost always deserted. It is now time to get back on the road to Harris, passing several scattered lochs along the way as the scenery becomes more hilly.

DAY 3: BETWEEN THE MOORLAND AND BEACHES OF HARRIS

Harris has two faces. To the east the Golden Road winds its way between rocky coves and isolated hamlets where a number of weaver's workshops carry on the traditions of Harris Tweed. Before exploring the west coast, dropping in for a bite to eat at Croft 36 is a must. This is a family-run, self-service bakery where you can treat yourself to soups, quiches, and small plates of crayfish, crab, and fish from Leverburgh. Then on to the vast beaches of Luskentyre, Traigh Seilebost, and Scarista, ribbons of white sand lapped by turquoise waters. The journey ends at the Harris Distillery, where gin and whisky made from the island's natural resources can be sampled—a last little sip of the Atlantic before heading for home.

LOST IN THE MIST

ISLE OF SKYE

The largest of the Inner Hebrides impresses in terms of both its beautiful and at times dramatic scenery and the uniqueness of its geological features.

P.132

The island's landscape consists of lochs, heather moors, and imposing peaks.

OPPOSITE

Skye's population numbers around ten thousand, around a third of whom speak Scots Gaelic.

The mountainous center of Skye, culminating in the peaks of the Black Cuillin ridge, extends out into a series of peninsulas whose jagged coastlines create scenery of dazzling beauty on a cinematic scale. It has been nicknamed the Misty Isle (possibly from the Old Norse *Skýey*), but its Gaelic name (*An t-Eilean Sgitheanach*) is thought to refer to its shape, looking a little like a wing extending from the west coast (*sgiath* means "wing"). Thanks to the Skye Bridge erected in 1995 over Loch Alsh, the island is easy to reach, and while no longer a remote destination its 639 square miles (1,656 km^2) are still full of interesting places to discover.

The almost fairytale scenery of the Trotternish Peninsula and the summit of the Old Man of Storr have become iconic emblems of the island, but the cathedral-like proportions of Spar Cave and Coral Beach near Dunvegan with its white maerl "sand" (made of crushed calcified coral-like seaweed) are equally worth seeing—the island's geology is every bit as rich as its history.

People have lived on Skye since the Mesolithic period, and the island has changed hands over the centuries, from the Celtic tribes and the Vikings to the clans MacDonald and MacLeod. Dunvegan Castle, overlooking an inlet of Loch Dunvegan, was built by the MacLeods and dates back to the thirteenth century. The island was under Norwegian rule until 1266, when it was transferred to Scotland under the terms of the Treaty of Perth. Skye was not spared the Highland Clearances inflicted by major landowners after the final Jacobite Rebellion of 1745, and many islanders were evicted from their homes and forced to emigrate elsewhere as the land was cleared for sheep farming. This was to halve the island's population.

While still far lower than in the eighteenth century, the population of Skye has been bouncing back thanks to those promoting the island's reputation through their work, such as chefs, farmers, fishermen, potters, and other artisans, helping the island to get back in touch with its Gaelic identity. Local restaurant tables overflow with scallops, crayfish, and vegetables, all caught or cultivated in the vicinity, along with the salt and various herbs also produced on the island.

Most of the good restaurants are in Portree, the capital (although you won't regret a short trip out of town to dine at Loch Bay, the Three Chimneys, or Kinloch Lodge). This small harbor town with its pastel-colored houses is a very pleasant spot and the perfect place in which to browse cafés and stores before setting off to see the island's natural wonders.

THE ESSENTIALS

PORTREE

The island's capital is well-known for its rows of colorful houses beside the waterfront. This former fishing port is now a lively town of stores, cafés, and restaurants, and is a departure point for boat trips

36

DUNTULM CASTLE

The ruins of the castle can be seen perched high on a cliff overlooking the sea in the north part of the island.

37

THE FAIRY GLEN

A scenic valley of green hills and rock formations, the Fairy Glen also lies in the north part of Skye.

38

NEIST POINT

At the westernmost tip of the Isle of Skye, a lighthouse on top of steep cliffs looks out over the Atlantic Ocean.

39

FAIRY POOLS

Streams flow down from the Cuillin Mountains to form these crystal-clear pools of turquoise water.

40

OLD MAN OF STORR

This famous rock formation looks out over the Trotternish Peninsula.

41

DUNVEGAN CASTLE AND GARDENS

The ancestral castle of Clan MacLeod is surrounded by magnificent gardens on the shores of Loch Dunvegan.

42

DUNSCAITH CASTLE

Another castle with a fine view from a windswept cliff, this time the remnants of a medieval fortress.

ABOVE

Volcanic hills, grazing land, and ferns form the landscape of the Fairy Glen near Uig.

OPPOSITE

The Fairy Glen is an otherworldly place, a landscape in miniature with hills and geological features shaped by erosion.

FOOD AND DRINK

JORDAN WEBB

A CHEF IN SYNC WITH NATURE

Composing menus based on what can be foraged and harvested in the immediate vicinity, chef Jordan Webb is in seventh heaven on the Isle of Skye. At Kinloch Lodge he offers sophisticated cuisine guided by this philosophy of self-sufficiency and the resources provided by nature.

When Jordan Webb arrived on the Isle of Skye in 2020 to lend a hand to the kitchen brigade at Kinloch Lodge (where work had been disrupted by the Covid pandemic), he thought he would only be staying for a matter of weeks. Five years on and Jordan is still here, running a restaurant that ranks among the best in Scotland; he simply never left. It represented a completely new chapter in the life of this globetrotter from South England, who had traveled the world from Canada to Japan. By joining this family enterprise steeped in history, Jordan has found his refuge and left his mark.

Kinloch Lodge was built here sometime in the seventeenth century, originally as a farm that was later converted into a hunting lodge. Its buildings of limewashed walls, topped with a slate roof in traditional Highland style, were transformed into a hotel in 1972. This was when Godfrey and Claire Macdonald resolved to create somewhere that lived up to their ideals of hospitality, with comfortable beds, friendly and attentive service, and—most importantly—delicious food. Claire, who was in charge of the restaurant, had to work with the limited deliveries from the mainland that arrived only every two weeks, so was already beginning to use produce from the surrounding countryside to compose her dishes.

Kinloch Lodge enjoys an excellent location on the shores of Loch na Dal, surrounded by hills and forest, as Jordan Webb is well aware. When not at his stove, the chef is to be found beside the waters of the loch, out in the forest, or in the hoop houses that he erected when he arrived. Under his watchful eye, wild strawberries, gooseberries, potatoes, and carrots have all been thriving here under cover. Gathering his own chanterelles in the forest and harvesting kelp (a local seaweed with underrated beneficial qualities) on the shores of the loch, Jordan is not just a chef-gardener but also a chef-forager.

Nature dictates the menu for Jordan and his team each day. They have close ties with local producers, providing access to crayfish, mussels, scallops, and venison from the Isle of Skye. Jeff, Jordan's long-time business partner, combs Scotland for whatever else is required, returning every two weeks with his precious finds, which the the chef then incorporates into dishes as only he can. Most recently, they have been using elderflower. Jordan is in tune with the island and its weather, but is also inspired by the mood of the moment, cooking vibrant and dynamic dishes that are deeply rooted in their surroundings.

1 / 3 / UNDER COVER

Chef Jordan Webb's hoop houses grow vegetables, berries, and herbs.

2 / SEASONALITY

The menu changes with the seasons, depending on what fresh produce can be caught or foraged.

4 / HISTORIC SURROUNDINGS

Kinloch Lodge has, by turns, been a farm, hunting lodge, and hotel.

5 / JORDAN WEBB

Having traveled the world, Jordan finally found a cure for his itchy feet on the Isle of Skye.

ABOVE

The Isle of Skye fosters a close relationship between people, the land, and the coastline.

OPPOSITE

The open pastureland on the Isle of Skye still supports a tranquil, rural lifestyle in tune with the slow rhythms of the seasons.

DULSE & BROSE

ABOVE

Portree, the island's capital, is not short of welcoming cafés and restaurants.

OPPOSITE

*According to one theory, Portree (*Port Rìgh *in Gaelic, the "port of the king") owes its name to a visit made by King James V of Scotland in 1540.*

ARTS AND CRAFTS

SKÍŌ POTTERY

POTTERS ON THE EDGE

From their workshop looking out to sea at the northern end of the Isle of Skye, Kayti Peschke and Luke Seaton create small batch ceramics inspired by the landscapes of the Hebrides.

The Waternish Peninsula is a well-kept secret, but it is here on this small stretch of land at the northwestern tip of Skye, pointing the way across the water to Lewis and Harris, that Kayti and Luke have found a haven. The couple (along with Frank, their miniature dachshund) have settled in a house with a stunning panoramic view looking out over the bay and the island of Isay. They set up their workshop in an architect-designed wooden shed next to their house and Skíō Pottery was founded in the winter of 2023.

Their story starts in the northern English city of York, where they met. Luke was running a pub and Kayti was a photographer, but even by then her passion for the decorative arts had already led her to try out a number of disciplines. Pottery was her favorite and she learned the basics from workshops and online videos. She then resolved to teach herself, experimenting and making plenty of mistakes. Taking his cue from Kayti, Luke also discovered the joy of making things with his hands, so the couple decided to write a new chapter in their story.

Their many holidays on the Isle of Skye conjured up the beguiling dream of settling down there one day—Kayti loved the sea, Luke loved mountains, and this particular island in the Inner Hebrides has plenty of both, so the couple decided to set up their studio here. The first glimpse of the extensive view from the large bay windows leaves you in no doubt that nature is their main source of inspiration—the jagged outlines of the peaks of the Black Cuillin are inscribed into the black clay of beakers and the texture of sandy beaches is recreated in the mottled beige clay of their mugs. Kayti and Luke sometimes also press patterns into the clay, using seashells picked up from the sand, such as at Coral Beach, one of the most beautiful on the island.

Orders from local restaurants came in thick and fast as soon as they set up shop, with the Michelin-starred Loch Bay—located just a mile up the road from Skíō Pottery in the fishing village of Stein—being one of the first to order some custom-made pieces. Skíō crockery is also in use in The Dunvegan, their favorite restaurant, and at Talisker, the local distillery. In addition to breathtaking surroundings, Luke and Kayti have also found a real community on the Isle of Skye and their work, shaped by wind, sea, and mountains, has become part of the history shared by the island's craft workers and restaurateurs.

INSPIRATION

Kayti and Luke are constantly inspired by Skye's unique environment, such as the white "sand" of Coral Beach.

CAREFUL CREATION

Their ceramic collections are produced in short runs, inspired by their appetite for creativity and to fulfill commissions.

ABOVE

The Dunvegan is a cozy restaurant that is popular with many locals.

OPPOSITE

A boat trip on Loch Dunvegan is a perfect opportunity to spot seals and seabirds.

ABOVE

The village of Ardvasar on the south coast is the last place to stop off for a drink before boarding the ferry.

OPPOSITE

All aboard the ferry that runs between Armadale on the Isle of Skye and Mallaig on the west coast of the Scottish mainland.

ARTISAN CRAFT

ISLE OF SKYE SEA SALT

TRADITIONAL SKILLS

A sustainable solar evaporation process is used to produce salt from the island's mineral-rich waters.

NATURAL ELEMENTS

The wind and the sun are all that are needed to produce this sea salt.

DRYING

Drying the salt can take four to eight weeks.

DRAINAGE

The drainage process is completed in a smaller drying tunnel, where the last traces of moisture evaporate.

LOCH WATER

The seawater from which the salt is produced is sourced from Loch Snizort and fed into shallow ponds.

EVAPORATION

The water evaporates slowly in the drying tunnels under the action of wind and sun.

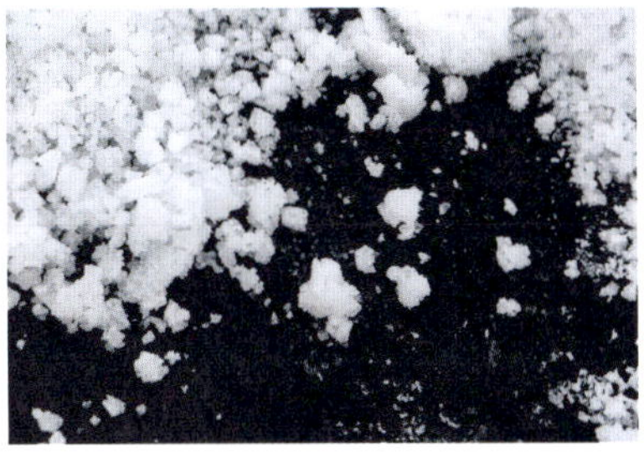

PRODUCTION CYCLE

The process is carried out in spring and summer.

AFTER HARVESTING

The salt is transferred to tubs to allow any remaining water to drain away.

ISLAND PRODUCE

A true produce of the island, the salt can be found in the best restaurants on Skye.

ABOVE

On the road to Neist Point, just beyond Loch Mòr.

OPPOSITE

Skye is around 50 miles (80 km) long and 25 miles wide (40 km), with a long coastline that is very diverse and indented.

With its sea link to the port at Mallaig on the mainland, the tranquil harbor of Ardvasar in the far south of the Isle of Skye is the gateway to the Sleat Peninsula.

DEEP DIVE

THE CASTLES AND MANOR HOUSES OF SCOTLAND

Perched on cliffs, looking out over a loch, or lost in the traditional swirling mist, castles are both part of the picture postcard image of Scotland and a picturesque reminder of the history of a nation.

The first castles were built in the twelfth century on the orders of King David I of Scotland, erected in the motte and bailey style that had been in use in England since the Norman Conquest of 1066. They consisted of a wooden keep constructed on a mound (the motte), surrounded by a palisaded enclosure (the bailey) that contained stables, living quarters, storehouses, and kitchens.

King David I ascended the Scottish throne in 1124 and invited Norman knights to build castles right across the country to protect the kingdom and secure power. Stone gradually supplanted wood, but these fortresses were put to the test during the Wars of Scottish Independence, which began in the late thirteenth century, becoming the scenes of violent clashes, traces of which are still visible to this day. They had been designed to withstand Viking raids but not the powerful armies of England, when the previously relatively cordial relations with Scotland's southern neighbors began to sour.

Castle design evolved over the centuries in response to military and technological advances. The arrival of gunpowder in the fourteenth century altered their construction, for example, prompting thicker walls and angular towers better able to withstand cannon fire. Castles were nonetheless to lose their defensive function over the course of the fifteenth century, morphing into tower houses and baronial manors. Stonework became more ornamental, gardens flourished, and the buildings became symbols of prestige and sophistication. Inspired by the French Renaissance, the seventeenth and eighteenth centuries saw the birth of a more elegant architectural style that still retained its Scottish traditional roots.

The appreciation of castles underwent a revival with the rise of the Romantic movement in the nineteenth century, and their picturesque ruins were celebrated by painters and writers. Queen Victoria fell in love with the Highlands and made Balmoral her Highland home, embracing a neo-baronial style with a mix of turrets and battlements that was to have a profound influence on Scottish architecture.

Today the landscape is still dotted with thousands of castles, manor houses, and ruins. Some are still occupied, others have been transformed into museums or hotels, while others again have been abandoned to the elements. All still live on in the country's memory, however.

EXTRAORDINARY HOMES

BALMORAL CASTLE

Balmoral is a private estate in Aberdeenshire belonging to the British monarchy.

INVERARAY CASTLE

In a stunning location on the shores of Loch Fyne, Inveraray Castle is the ancestral seat of the Clan Campbell.

CAWDOR CASTLE

A fortified residence inhabited for over six hundred years, Cawdor Castle with its central medieval tower is surrounded by gardens and extensive grounds.

LIVING AMID HISTORY

Scottish manor houses and castles are landmarks in the landscape, while the choice of their location, often strategic or symbolic, reflects a lasting relationship between architecture, land, and local identity.

ABOVE

Dunvegan Castle is the historic seat of Clan MacLeod on the Isle of Skye.

OPPOSITE

The castle has dominated the landscape overlooking the shores of Loch Dunvegan since the thirteenth century.

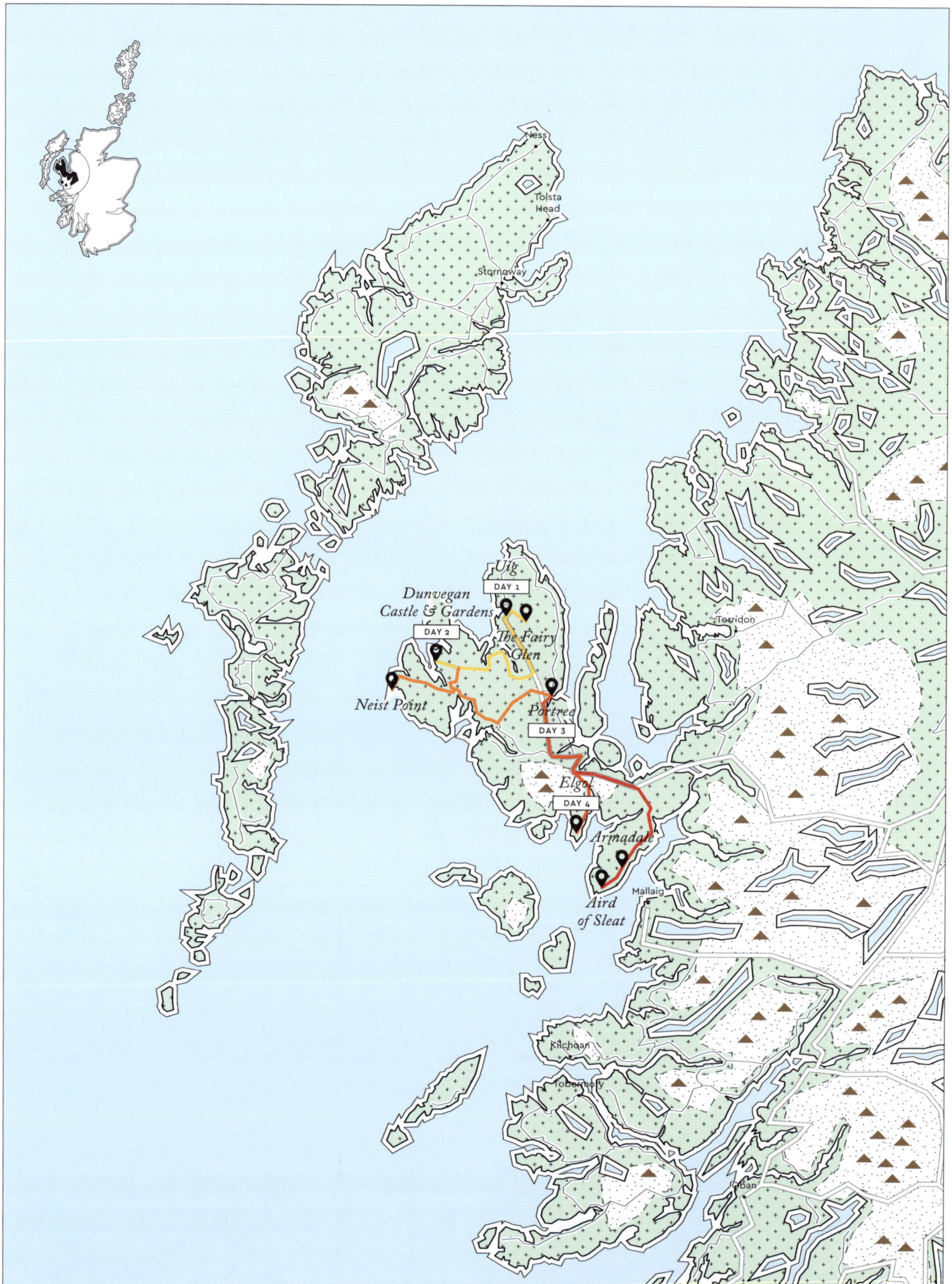
Ness
Tolsta Head
Stornoway
Uig
DAY 1
Dunvegan Castle & Gardens
DAY 2
The Fairy Glen
Neist Point
Portree
DAY 3
Torridon
Elgol
DAY 4
Armadale
Aird of Sleat
Mallaig
Kilchoan
Tobermory
Oban

EXCURSION

A TOUR OF THE ISLE OF SKYE

The most famous of the islands of the Inner Hebrides is known for its wild and dramatic scenery, the inspiration for many myths and legends. This tour from north to south is an ideal way to explore the most spectacular parts of the island.

DAY 1: THE TROTTERNISH PENINSULA

The ferry from Lewis and Harris to Skye docks at Uig in the north of the island. The spectacle begins as soon as you step off the boat to begin exploring the Trotternish Peninsula, home to the Fairy Glen. This is a magical valley enclosed by an enchanting succession of green conical hills, *lochans* (small lochs), and towers of rock such as Castle Ewen, a natural landmark formed of basalt. The Old Man of Storr, a little further to the south, is a pinnacle of rock 157 ft (48 m) high, with a distinctive outline that dominates the landscape. The path up to the rock is very steep, but offers fantastic views of the peninsula.

DAY 2: DUNVEGAN AND NEIST POINT LIGHTHOUSE

On the way to the northwestern tip of the island, stop off at Dunvegan Castle to learn about the history of Clan MacLeod, who have lived here since the thirteenth century. A boat trip around the islands of Loch Dunvegan is an excellent opportunity to catch a glimpse of the seals that live there. The road carries on for another 10 miles (17 km), revealing ever more breathtaking scenery around each bend. From the green, windswept headland of Neist Point, a steep path leads to the rocky promontory on which the lighthouse stands. Built in 1900, when it was staffed, it is one of the most famous in Scotland.

DAY 3: PORTREE AND THE MOUNTAINS OF THE BLACK CUILLIN

The third day of the tour takes in the island's capital, with its charming small harbor overlooking a sheltered bay bobbing with boats. After a quick stop for a snack at Birch, a café that roasts its own coffee, it is time to set off to tackle the mountains at the center of the island. The dark, jagged peaks of the dramatic Black Cuillin are a mecca for hikers. The Fairy Pools, at the foot of the mountains, are natural pools and waterfalls of crystal-clear water in striking contrast to the stark scenery of the mountains.

DAY 4: SOUTH OF THE ISLAND

The less well-traveled southern end of the island has a few well-kept secrets. At Egol a cathedral-like sea cave awaits intrepid adventurers bold enough to venture beneath the giant limestone columns carved out by the sea over centuries, beyond which lies the Mermaid Pool. Keep an eye on the tide tables, however. In the village of Armadale, not far from the ancient stones of Armadale Castle, the Museum of the Isles chronicles the history of the Highlands and the Clan MacDonald of Sleat, one of Skye's most prominent families. Nearing the end of the trip at Aird of Sleat, look for a small path leading to a secluded beach, a last chance to take a moment to contemplate the surrounding scenery before boarding the ferry for Mallaig and the mainland.

FROM PENINSULA TO LOCH

THE WEST COAST

From the Mull of Kintyre to Mallaig, the west coast bordering the Argyll and Bute region and the southwestern Highlands has a heavily indented coastline and craggy mountains dominated by the valley of Glen Coe.

P.164

The road along Glen Coe winds through some of the most dramatic mountainscapes in the Highlands.

OPPOSITE

Camusdarach Beach to the north of Arisaig is one of the most beautiful on this stretch of the coast.

Driving along the west coast, it seems as though there's a fabulous view around every corner. This is a wild landscape of secluded bays and beaches, green valleys, and towering mountains. The quality of the light here is special, adding to the sense of drama.

To the south Argyll alternates between glens (valleys) and lush forests. Take the A83 across the Arrochar Alps and through the famous Rest and Be Thankful pass, with its viewpoint, to reach Argyll Forest Park. Tucked away amid its lush greenery is Inveraray, once a royal burgh and the seat of the Dukes of Argyll since the fifteenth century; it is known for being a particularly attractive example of Scottish Georgian architecture. In 1746 Archibald Campbell, the third Duke of Argyll, chose to build a castle near the River Aray, but it required moving the small town of Inveraray and its inhabitants to its present location around half a mile away on the shore of Loch Fyne.

Oban (the name means "little bay" in Gaelic) lies around 30 miles (50 km) to the north. It has long been the maritime capital of the west coast. The arrival in the nineteenth century of the railroad helped to make Oban the gateway to the islands, with a ferry service from the town completing the journey to the Hebridean islands of Mull, Iona, Coll, and Barra. Cargoes of freshly landed fish and shellfish, which can be sampled right by the harborside, have made Oban famous throughout the country.

The landscape is even more dramatic further north, as the mountains close in around Glen Coe, a deep valley popular with mountaineers. However, behind this wild beauty lurks a dark tale—the 1692 massacre in which an estimated thirty-eight men, women, and children of Clan MacDonald were slaughtered by a company of soldiers belonging to the Campbells of Argyll who were loyal to English King James II. The most spectacular stretch of the West Highland Line begins at Fort William, a town in the shadow of Ben Nevis—the highest mountain in the country at 4,413 ft (1,345 m). The line winds its way through glens, skirting remote lochs, eventually crossing the legendary Glenfinnan Viaduct. The Jacobite Steam Train racing around the curve of the viaduct, smoke pouring from its chimney, must be one of Scotland's most iconic images.

On reaching Arisaig, the scenery becomes more mellow, with the coastal road leading past quiet bays and beaches of white sand backed by dunes, where a single ray of sunshine is all that is needed to turn the water a startling shade of turquoise.

THE ESSENTIALS

43

MALLAIG

This Highland fishing town is also a major seaport and the departure point for ferries to the Isle of Skye and the Inner Hebrides.

44

RHU POINT BEACH

The breathtaking scenery of this remote beach at the end of the Rhu Peninsula is a well-kept secret and is accessible only on foot.

45

ARISAIG

This pretty village on the banks of Loch nan Ceall makes a great base from which to explore the surrounding islands.

46

EASDALE

One of the Slate Islands, the gray of the slate rock is still visible everywhere in the landscape.

47

ISLE OF MULL

The second-largest island of the Inner Hebrides is home to a pretty, colorful harbor from where you can explore the island of Iona and its abbey.

48

GLENFINNAN

The viaduct with its steam train is one of Scotland's most famous images.

49

BEN NEVIS

With an elevation of 4,413 ft (1,345 m), Ben Nevis is the highest peak in the British Isles.

50

OBAN

The maritime capital of the west coast sees ferries and fishing boats crossing paths on a daily basis.

51

ARGYLL AND BUTE

This region extending along the west coast is bordered by Loch Lomond and the Trossachs to the east and has an impressive variety of scenery and a host of ruins.

52

CASTLE STALKER

Standing proudly on a rocky islet surrounded by water, the castle can be reached only at low tide.

53

INVERARAY

Who can resist the charm of the white facades of the houses here in the ancestral seat of the Dukes of Argyll?

54

THREE SISTERS OF GLEN COE

On a mountainous ridge, the Three Sisters look out over the green valley of Glen Coe.

ABOVE

The magnificent beach at Camusdarach between Arisaig and Mallaig is an inviting spot for a dip.

OPPOSITE

The expanses of fine sand, rocky coves filled with flowers, and grassy dunes of this wild beach are well worth exploring.

ARCHITECTURE

INVERLONAN

A DIFFERENT WAY OF LIVING IN NATURE

Nestling among the dense forests and remote lochs of the west coast of the Highlands, Inverlonan is reinventing the art of living off-grid and is where stripped-back simplicity meets epicurean indulgence.

Although just a few miles from Oban, Inverlonan is one of those places that requires a little bit of effort and that extra mile to reach. Once guests have parked their cars at the end of a winding road, the manager, Dee, loads them onto an all-terrain cart and drives them to Loch Nell, which is tucked away in the kind of wild natural setting that only Scotland can offer. It is here, hidden away in a forest of ancient oaks, that three modern bothies keep watch over the dark waters of the loch. Following in the footsteps of the traditional mountain refuges that are scattered across Scotland, they are reinventing the art of the bothy.

Taking their inspiration from Scandinavian design, the Bothy Stores social project founded by artist Bobby Niven and architect Iain MacLeod, has created a version of the shelters that blends tradition and modernity. Each hut features a small living area with a kitchen, mezzanine space accessible via a ladder, a private terrace, an outdoor stove, and a wood-fired pizza oven. The bothies are completely off-grid, with no connection to mains power, gas, or running water. There is an outdoor shower, and the amenities are rounded off with eco-friendly rest rooms, adding comfort without compromising the minimalist esthetic.

The Inverlonan bothies have been designed for the present but were inspired by the past, as an opportunity to change down a gear, observe, and rethink our relationship with our resources. Days here pass with walks in the forest, canoe trips on the loch, relaxing in the sauna, and cooking over an open fire. Dee is in charge of bringing carefully curated provisions from local producers to the door, and the food is then prepared in the open air. The magical view over Loch Nell lends the whole adventure a very special feel.

Once night has fallen, guests take their place at chef Tim Kensett's table in the forest. Tim provides an eight-course menu cooked over an open fire. Creating dishes from ingredients that could not be fresher, more local, or more seasonal, he has proved that gastronomy can shake off the rules and operate off-grid—a unique experience that takes us right back to basics.

1 / 4 / MODERN SHELTER

Uisge Bothy overlooking Loch Nell provides the opportunity to slow down the pace of life in absolute tranquility.

2 / 3 / OPEN-AIR KITCHEN

All the cooking here is done over an open fire using local produce.

5 / COMFORT AND SIMPLICITY

Despite the absence of running water and electricity, modern comforts are not totally forgotten.

ABOVE

Long summer evenings while staying in one of the bothies at Inverlonan are spent around the fire, with the loch as a backdrop.

OPPOSITE

Every aspect of the bothies' interiors has been designed to take guests back to greater simplicity and reconnect with the environment.

DEEP DIVE

SCOTTISH MYTHS AND LEGENDS

Scotland is a land of oral tradition, preserving its stories down the centuries thanks to its folklorists, poets, and writers.

A thick mist over the loch, the ruins of a castle on the brow of a cliff, wild horses roaming the dunes—reality merges with imagination in the landscapes of Scotland. A long oral tradition has ensured that tales and legends have survived down the centuries, stories from Celtic and Gaelic traditions handed from generation to generation by storytellers and bards (*seanchaidh* in Gaelic) long before they were ever written down.

In such stories, the natural world is populated by gods, spirits, phantoms, and witches. The kelpie, a water sprite in the form of a horse-like creature, lures unwary travelers into the depths of the lochs, while the selkie, shifting shape from human to seal form, originates on the island shores of Orkney. Morag is a lake monster said to swim in the waters of Loch Morar, while the territory of Nessie, Morag's far better known cousin, is of course Loch Ness, and on stormy nights, you might even hear the melancholy skirl of the ghostly piper of Culzean Castle.

The origins of some locations are even attributed to legends. Fingal's Cave on the uninhabited island of Staffa, for example, is said to be all that is left of a bridge across the sea between Scotland and Northern Ireland. It was built by a giant so that he could fight his rival from over the water. From a geological perspective, Fingal's Cave was formed from basalt columns left by a lava flow, similar in structure to the Giant's Causeway in Northern Ireland.

Poets and writers, from James Macpherson to Sir Walter Scott, started to write these stories down in the eighteenth century, ensuring that this essentially oral folklore tradition would be passed on. One such poet was Robert Burns, regarded as Scotland's national poet. His poem "Tam O'Shanter" is well known in Scotland and tells the story of a farmer who spends an evening having a little too much to drink and then spies witches, wizards, and even Auld Nick (Old Nick, aka the devil) himself as he walks home past the haunted church of Alloway Auld Kirk in Ayr. James Matthew (JM) Barrie was a playwright and novelist, but is best known for being the creator of Peter Pan in the magical children's tale, originally a play, *Peter Pan, or the Boy Who Wouldn't Grow Up*.

This heritage continues to be preserved to this day in literature, museums, and in festivals of storytelling ... and the legends continue to populate Scottish imagination. It should therefore come as no surprise to learn that Scotland's national animal is a mythological beast—the unicorn is a symbol of purity, independence, and power.

A LEGENDARY BESTIARY

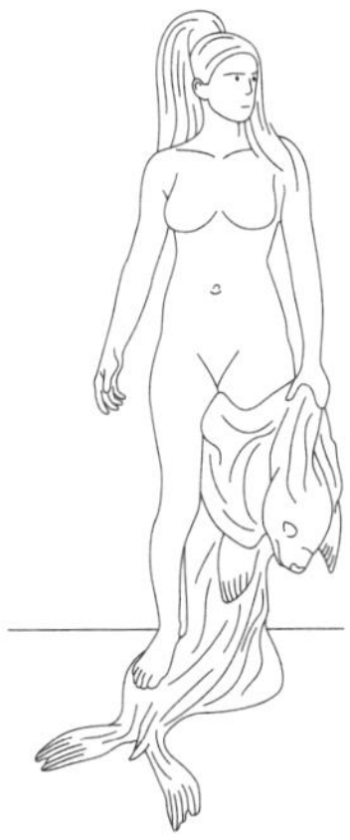

SELKIE

The selkie features in the folklore of the Northern Isles and is a seal capable of shedding its skin to take on human form.

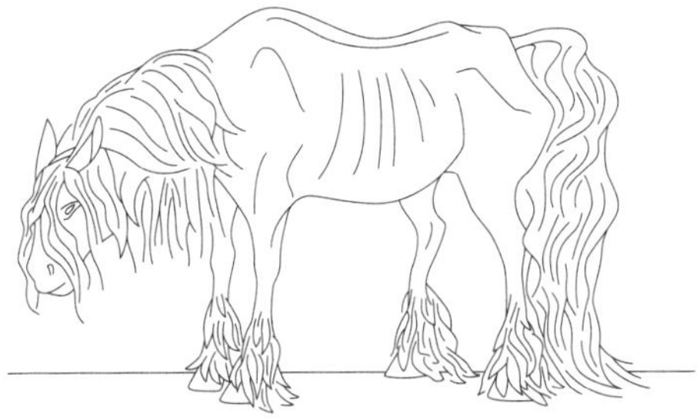

KELPIE

Kelpies are water spirits inhabiting lakes and rivers. With the appearance of a horse, they carry off and drown all those who try to mount them.

NUCKELAVEE

The first tales of the nuckelavee originate in Orkney and tell of a hybrid, fleshless creature both human and equine. It is associated with epidemics and failed harvests.

MORAG

Sightings of Morag, a gigantic, serpentine creature, have been reported in Loch Morar since the nineteenth century—just one of the freshwater monsters regularly sighted around Scotland.

*It is hardly surprising that such a landscape might spark myths and legends;
any number of malevolent spirits could be lurking in its caves and rocky nooks and crannies.*

ABOVE

The building housing the Argyll and Bute archives is visible through a window from Inveraray Castle.

OPPOSITE

Although the castle has been occupied by Clan Campbell since the fifteenth century, the current building dates back to the second half of the eighteenth century.

The pretty town of Inveraray lies along the shores of Loch Fyne in Argyll and Bute.

The rows of whitewashed houses in Inveraray are a fine example of Scottish Georgian architecture.

FOOD AND DRINK

INVER RESTAURANT

A CULINARY HAVEN ON THE WEST COAST

Chef Pamela (Pam) Brunton offers her unique approach to food and accommodation opposite the centuries-old Lachlan Castle on the banks of Loch Fyne.

From the shores of the North Sea to the coastline of the Atlantic, Pamela Brunton has long followed her instincts. Having grown up in Carnoustie, a small town on Scotland's eastern seaboard, she moved to the west coast at the age of twenty-one, a friend having told her about a job in the kitchen of a seafood restaurant where the friend was working. Pamela accepted the job and has never stopped cooking since. After ten years on the London restaurant scene, a chance visit to friends living on the Isle of Iona opened up a whole new horizon for her. The owner of a hotel restaurant was looking for a chef for the season and Pamela sized her chance. Her partner Rob Latimer thought it might be an opportunity to try his hand at front-of-house, and an internship at Noma won him over. He quit his job as a motion designer to follow her on this adventure.

The couple began to dream of a restaurant of their own but searched for a site in vain. They eventually had another stroke of luck when a friend told them about a restaurant (a former crofter's cottage on the banks of Loch Fyne) that was about to become available. The opportunity was too good to let slip—Pamela and Rob seized it with both hands and Inver opened its doors in 2015. Being suddenly so far from the madding crowd of the big cities, Pamela had to reinvent the way she cooked. Above all, she had to establish links with the local community, which would be key to settling in. The meetings she had with producers gradually swelled the menu and forged new personal connections. She still remembers the winter evening when the restaurant was almost entirely filled with the local producers whose produce was being served on the plates in front of them. A memorable occasion that perfectly encapsulated the spirit of the place.

At Inver Pamela has discovered the true meaning of sustainable cooking and sets out her vision of the links that unite people with the landscapes that surround them in her book *Between Two Waters*. She highlights the entire chain of cooperation and collaboration that is essential to producing the meals on our plates, from the insects in the soil to the aquatic life in the loch, from the gardener to the farmer, and from the fisherman to the ghillie. She also questions the things that influence what we eat—from gender to capitalism and colonialism, not to mention cultural and personal background.

Her work earned her a Michelin Green Star in 2021 (making Inver one of the first restaurants in Scotland to win such an honor). Guests also have the option to stay overnight in one of the on-site bothies and shepherd's huts (all designed by Pamela's architect father), providing an experience where land, people, and cuisine all come together.

At first sight, Inver looks like a charming family home.

Inside, the parquet flooring and wooden furniture create a warm ambience.

Every room has large bay windows looking out over rich vegetation.

The chef aims to combine food, sustainability, and landscape on a plate.

Pamela Brunton has been living on the shores of Loch Fyne since 2015.

Pamela is exploring the way we eat, from where food is sourced to where it is prepared.

Travelers can deepen their experience of the surroundings by staying in one of the bothies.

Diners can explore the local landscape and produce through homemade dishes.

The restaurant enjoys the tranquility of Loch Fyne and offers visitors a taste of nature.

ISLE OF LEWIS
GLASGOW

ABOVE

The Oban Seafood Hut on the harborside at Oban is just the place to try freshly landed seafood and shellfish.

OPPOSITE

The ferries ply the route to the Hebrides.

SLATE ISLAND

EASDALE ISLANDS

GETTING AWAY FROM IT ALL

HISTORY

Easdale was a major center of slate production in Scotland until the nineteenth century.

SEIL

Easdale is a small island with no roads or cars, accessible only by ferry from Seil, another of the Slate Islands.

COMMUNITY

The small community that now lives on the island has renovated the former workers' cottages.

ELLENABEICH

A ferry leaves the village of Ellenabeich on Seil, opposite Easdale, every thirty minutes.

HERITAGE

The slate was used on roofs right across the United Kingdom and even further afield.

RICOCHETS

The World Stone Skimming Championship is held annually at the town's quarry pools.

RUINS

Easdale was almost entirely abandoned after the slate industry collapsed.

SLATE MINING

The old quarries have now been flooded but still mark the island's landscape.

ABOVE

A sign shows the way to the remote beach at Port Nam Murrach, just south of Arisaig.

OPPOSITE

Seals take some time out on one of the rocky islets around Arisaig.

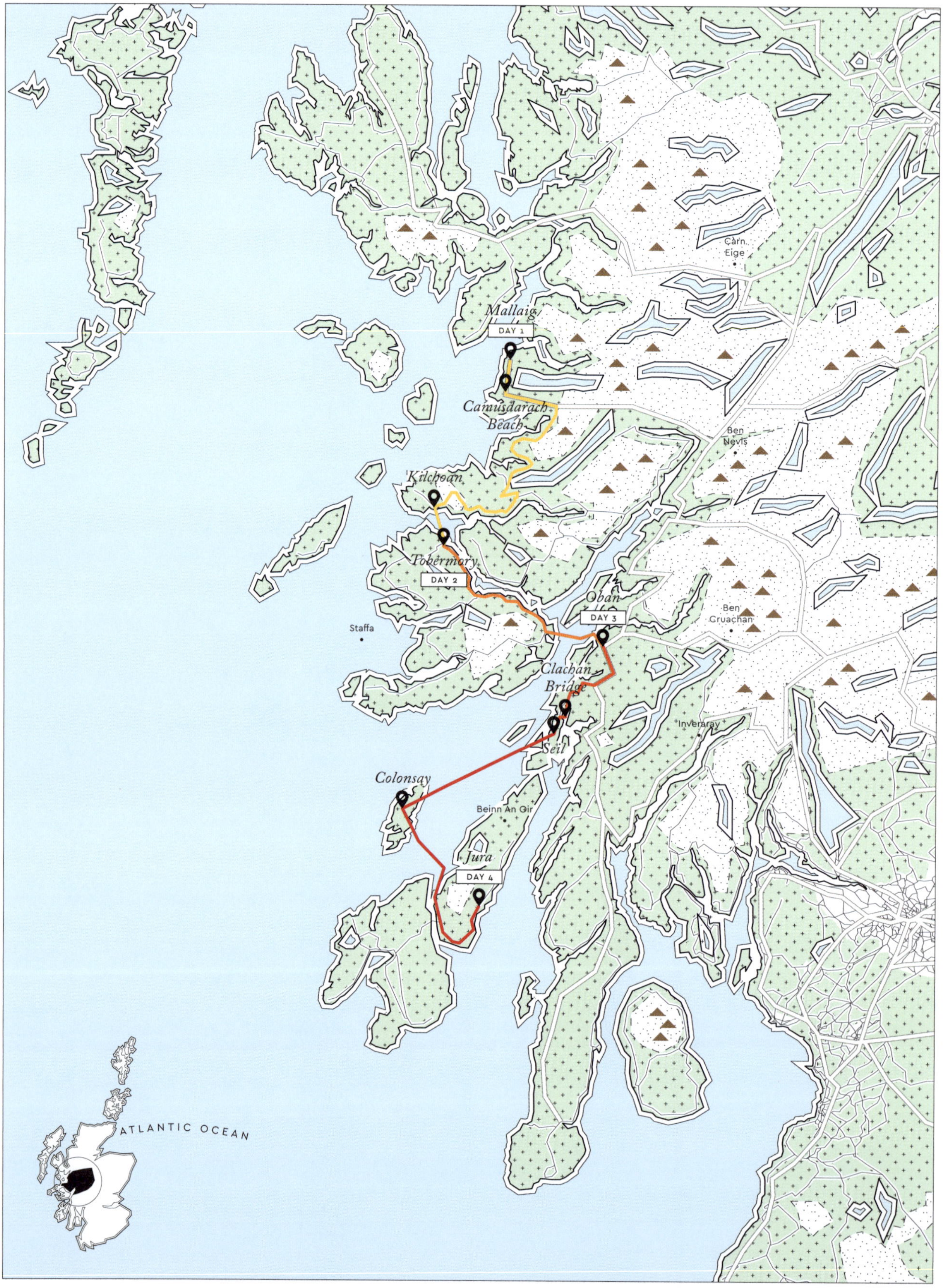
Carn Eige
Mallaig
DAY 1
Camusdarach Beach
Ben Nevis
Kilchoan
Tobermory
DAY 2
Oban
DAY 3
Ben Cruachan
Staffa
Clachan Bridge
Inveraray
Seil
Colonsay
Beinn An Oir
Jura
DAY 4
ATLANTIC OCEAN

EXCURSION

ISLAND HOPPING ON THE WEST COAST

Leaving Mallaig, the A830 coast road winds its way between a series of peninsulas to reveal a rocky coastline punctuated by beaches of white sand. A whole host of islands lying offshore invite you to stop off to experience island life.

DAY 1: MALLAIG AND THE SMALL ISLES

The first stop on a tour of the islands is Camusdarach beach, near Mallaig, undoubtedly one of the most beautiful in Scotland. The contrast between the sky and the ever-shifting light here adds to the poetic quality of the location. From Mallaig look west to see Rùm and Eigg, two of the four islands in the Small Isle archipelago. Rùm is now a National Nature Reserve, home to volcanic peaks, red deer, and white-tailed eagles; Eigg is smaller but has a thriving community. The blackhouses of the deserted village of Grulin on Eigg stand in the shadow of An Sgùrr, the highest point on the island.

DAY 2: THE ISLANDS OF MULL AND STAFFA

Accessible by ferry from Kilchoan, Mull really has it all—beaches and bays of turquoise water, dense forests, a coastline of dramatic scenery and rugged mountains. Tobermory is the capital whose colorful houses feature in many a smartphone photo. It is a great place to sample seafood and to find a bed for the night, but many visitors also make for the natural cliff formations of the Carsaig Arches. The more adventurous will also want to see the spectacular Fingal's Cave on the neighboring Isle of Staffa, also a National Nature Reserve. This is a natural cavern with amazing acoustics, where hundreds of hexagonal basalt columns rise up from the sea. A colony of puffins is in residence here over the summer.

DAY 3: OBAN AND THE ISLE OF SEIL

The tour continues south to Oban, a major port known as the Gateway to the Isles and the departure point for ferries to much of the Hebrides. Climb the hill to McCaig's Tower (an unfinished replica of the Coliseum in Rome) for a beautiful bird's-eye panorama of Oban Bay. At the harborside visitors can try mussels, oysters, and lobster, freshly landed from the fishing boats and cooked at the famous Oban Seafood Hut (the Green Shack). The small Clachan Bridge (the "Bridge over the Atlantic") just to the south links the west coast of the mainland with the island of Seil where you'll find a fishing village full of picturesque white cottages.

DAY 4: JURA AND ISLAY

The islands of Jura and Islay can also be reached by ferry from Oban via Colonsay. Islay, known as the Queen of the Hebrides is renowned among lovers of single malt whisky for its ten distilleries, all of which are still in operation. The Isle of Jura is wilder but equally dedicated to whisky production, despite a significant wildlife population that includes a herd of deer that outnumbers the human inhabitants! A stop with a difference to round off this island-hopping excursion.

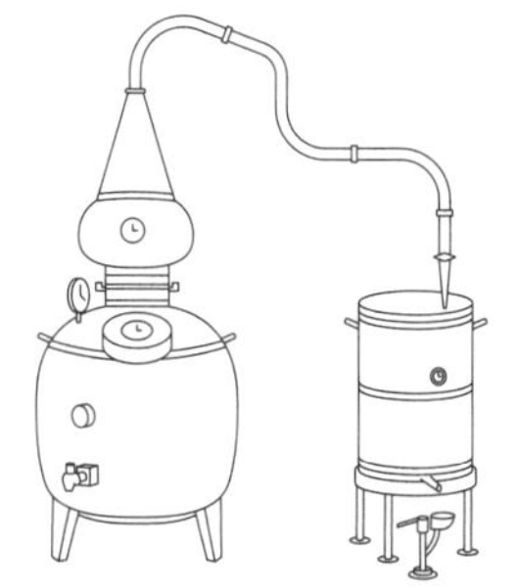

A CITY OF CREATIVITY

IN AND AROUND GLASGOW

Glasgow, Scotland's largest city, has evolved over the centuries and today is a modern city bursting with creativity in which music plays a very special role. It is also the ideal starting point for excursions to the Trossachs, the Isle of Arran, and the Dumfries and Galloway region.

P.194

Kelvingrove Art Gallery and Museum, designed by Charles Rennie Mackintosh, is a typical example of Glasgow Style architecture.

OPPOSITE

A colorful bar on the Great Western Road in northwestern Glasgow.

The city's history began when sixth-century Christian missionary St Mungo built the church on the banks of the Clyde that was later to become the cathedral we see today. However, the real boom in Glasgow's fortunes took place much later, at the turn of the nineteenth century, when the Industrial Revolution transformed it into a major center for manufacturing, mineral ore production, international trade, and shipbuilding. Unsanitary working-class tenements sprang up to house Irish immigrants and Highland farmers who had been forced to leave their homesteads.

The industrial decline that began in the 1960s forced the closure of the shipyards (that had launched the *Queen Mary* and *Queen Elizabeth* ocean liners) and many of the city's factories. The smoke of industry cleared, derelict tenements were razed to the ground, and Glasgow became a playground for celebrity architects. The SEC Armadillo Auditorium (formerly the Clyde Auditorium), designed by Sir Norman Foster, and Zaha Hadid's Riverside Museum were added to the buildings in the Glasgow Style already scattered throughout the city. A Scottish take on art nouveau, Glasgow Style was introduced by Charles Rennie Mackintosh at the end of the nineteenth century and is visible all over the city, from the splendid Glasgow School of Art to the Kelvingrove Art Gallery and Museum.

Glasgow was designated European City of Culture for 1990, and has since become inextricably linked to the designers, architects, artists, and musicians who have turned the city into a vibrant and creative melting pot. Music is of particular importance and in 2008 Glasgow became the third city in the world to be named a "UNESCO City of Music," with more than a hundred concerts and similar performances taking place every week. The Royal Scottish National Orchestra is just one of the many organizations headquartered here.

Glasgow's location in the heart of the Clyde Valley is every bit as convenient in terms of accessibility as Edinburgh's at the eastern end of Scotland's Central Belt area. From Glasgow, in just under two hours by car, you could be exploring the rolling countryside of Dumfries and Galloway or a condensed version of the Scottish landscape on the Isle of Arran. Better still, head north to the banks of Loch Lomond and the majestic Loch Lomond & The Trossachs National Park.

THE Hug AND PINT
THE Hug AND PINT
171 Great Western Rd

THE ESSENTIALS

55

ASHTON LANE

An iconic thoroughfare in Glasgow's West End, with a movie theater and a host of bars and restaurants.

56

GEORGE SQUARE

A number of statues (including one of the poet Robert Burns) now stand in Glasgow's main square, which was named in honor of King George III.

57

GLASGOW BOTANIC GARDENS

Glasgow's Botanic Gardens were opened in 1817 and include a magnificent Victorian glasshouse.

58

UNIVERSITY OF GLASGOW

Scotland's second-oldest university is well worth a visit for its Gothic Revival architecture and cloisters.

59

DUKE OF WELLINGTON STATUE

This equestrian statue on Royal Exchange Square in 1844 has become famous thanks to the traffic cone that has been placed on the duke's head.

60

BARRAS MARKET

A popular and lively market that has been an institution since the beginning of the twentieth century. Come here to browse antiques, discount clothing, and food.

61

KELVINGROVE ART GALLERY AND MUSEUM

The Kelvingrove combines art, history, and science in a magnificent Spanish Baroque building opened in 1901.

62

THE TALL SHIP GLENLEE

A historic sailing ship launched in 1896 and now moored on the River Clyde, this steel three-masted barque once transported freight all over the world before being converted into a training ship.

63

THE CLYDE RIVER

Glasgow's river is closely tied up with the city's industrial and maritime history.

64

RIVERSIDE MUSEUM

This transport and technology museum has more than three thousand exhibits (from skateboards to music equipment) housed in a contemporary building on the banks of the Clyde.

65

LOCH LOMOND & THE TROSSACHS

The first national park created in Scotland extends all the way from the Southern Highlands to North Glasgow, bisected by one of the longest freshwater lochs in the country.

66

LUSS

This pretty conservation village on the banks of Loch Lomond with neat rows of cottages and a pier is a popular stop.

P.200–201

From medieval ruins to Victorian Gothic masterpieces and contemporary architecture, Glasgow tells the tale of its history through its buildings.

ABOVE

The University of Glasgow was founded in 1451 and is now one of the most renowned universities in the country.

OPPOSITE

Built in the Scottish Gothic style, it is one of the finest buildings in the city.

DRINK

THE CLYDESIDE DISTILLERY

THE ART OF SCOTCH WHISKY

The Clydeside Distillery on the banks of the Clyde is reconnecting Glasgow with its history through its single malt whisky, right here in the heart of the city.

With its red stone building topped with a clock tower and an extension of glass and steel, the architecture of the Clydeside Distillery embodies its ambition to modernize a historic tradition. Morrison Glasgow Distillers found the ideal site for their project in the old Pump House of Queen's Dock. It was here in the old pumping station that the hydraulic power required to operate the dock's swing bridge was once generated, allowing freighters loaded with barrels of whisky to pass through. They were unaware at the time that John Morrison, a direct ancestor, had been involved in the construction of these very shipyards in 1863, a coincidence that added a considerable symbolic dimension.

The story of the Morrison family's links with whisky began in the early 1900s. Just half a century later, Stanley P. Morrison was enjoying a successful career as a broker specializing in Scottish spirits when, in 1963, he learned that the Bowmore Distillery, the oldest on the Isle of Islay, had been put up for sale. He bought it the very same day and his family suddenly found themselves in the business of whisky production. Glen Garioch, near Aberdeen, was next on the shopping list, followed by Auchentoshan, in North Glasgow, all of which were then united under the name of Morrison Bowmore Distillers.

By 2017 it was the turn of the Clydeside Distillery to open its doors and join the movement aimed at bringing single malt whisky distilling back to Glasgow. Although hundreds of distilleries were operating in the city in the nineteenth century, those that produced whisky were the first victims of closures in the century that followed, eventually disappearing from the urban landscape. Single malts were not to return to Glasgow until the Glasgow Distillery opened in 2012. Unlike a blended whisky, where multiple kinds of grain can be used in production, a single malt uses only malted barley and comes from a single distillery (in which the various casks may be blended to give each its own character).

Staying true to this tradition, the Clydeside Distillery is once again crafting whisky using water from Loch Katrine, which has been the main source of fresh water for Glasgow for more than a hundred and fifty years. The construction firm of another member of the Morrison family, John Morrison, was involved in the work that originally turned the loch into a reservoir. By connecting the loch to the Clydesdale Distillery on the banks of the river, the distillery completes the circle, binding together more than a century of Glasgow history with the Morrison family and the River Clyde.

MODERNIZATION

A contemporary building made entirely of glass and housing two copper stills now stands beside the clock tower and pumphouse built in 1877.

A WEE DRAM

Stobcross, the first release from the Clydeside Distillery, is a single malt whisky aged in bourbon casks.

BEER - WINE - TEQUILA - RUM
LUPE PINTOS DELI
MEXICAN
SPANISH
AMERICAN
HELLZAPOPPIN'
PRINTS

ABOVE

Many of Glasgow's buildings were built of a red sandstone imported mainly from Dumfriesshire and Ayrshire at the beginning of the twentieth century.

OPPOSITE

The best way to get to know Glasgow is through its restaurants, cafés, delis, bars, and—of course—its music venues.

ABOVE

Scotland's culinary specialties include the Scotch egg, which can even be made with haggis in place of the traditional sausage meat casing.

OPPOSITE

Café Gandolfi is a real institution and an integral part of the city's history.

COVE CAFE
LE RENDEZVOUS
WILLS
UNIVERSITY CAFE

VISIT

THE ISLE OF ARRAN

SCOTLAND IN MINIATURE

Situated in the Firth of Clyde, Arran may be only 20 miles (32 km) long and 10 miles (16 km) wide, but it is like Scotland in microcosm, a place where you can see all the different kinds of scenery that Scotland has to offer without leaving the island's shores. The best way to explore Arran is by following a 55-mile (88-km) loop around the coast.

The Isle of Arran, just a one-hour ferry ride from Glasgow (departing from Ardrossan), has a unique geology. The island was formed more than 60 million years ago at a time when Scotland and North America were slowly being separated by the formation of the North Atlantic Ocean. The majestic granite mountains in the northern part of the island also date from this period, including Goat Fell, its highest point at 2,867 ft (874 m). The Highland Boundary Fault Line, which marks the natural border between the Highlands and the Lowlands, runs from the Isle of Arran in the west (and terminates in Stonehaven in the east). This explains the variety of the island's scenery, with rolling hills to the south and granite peaks to the north, and has also resulted in its designation as a UNESCO Global Geopark in 2025.

The Vikings also left their mark. Brodick, the island's capital, takes its name from Old Norse *breidavik* ("wide bay"), testament to several centuries of Norse rule between the nineth and thirteenth centuries. Scotland did not in fact take possession of Arran until the defeat of the Vikings at the Battle of Largs in 1263, and although the island's fate hung in the balance during the Anglo-Scottish Wars, it was ultimately to remain within the Scottish fold.

These days the island has retained a strong identity underpinned by the dynamism of its inhabitants. Located here are two award-winning whisky distilleries (Lagg and Lochranza), a wide choice of bistros, and a host of stores and galleries, not to mention a past with a legacy of numerous cairns and chambered tombs dating back to the Bronze Age, along with menhirs and rock carvings.

Take the road south to find Eas Mòr, a stunning waterfall in the surrounding forest, and the Library in the Woods (where passers-by pin up their poems in a small cottage), while the cliffs of basalt rock concealing King's Cave are found to the east. Turn north and you are likely to spot some seals in the water offshore. In Lochranza village, a stop at the Sandwich Station is a must before exploring Glen Sannox, where the scenery and herds of red deer epitomize the spirit of the glens.

A tour around the island is finally completed in the charming village of Corrie on the north coast with a stop at Brodick Beach, where the Cladach Beach House serves locally brewed and distilled cocktails infused with island herbs such as lemon balm, sea lettuce, and wild thyme. They are delicious enjoyed on the beach in summer, right by the water's edge, or warmed by the wood-burning stove in winter.

Cladach Beach House creates cocktails with botanical infusions made from Arran's plants.

The rocky beaches on the west coast are home to seals and seabirds.

The village of Corrie is one of the most picturesque on the island.

The ruins of Lochranza Castle stand on a narrow headland.

Foot passengers as well as vehicles take the ferry from Ardrossan to Arran.

Taking the road around the island is the perfect way to enjoy the variety of scenery.

Lochranza Distillery in the northern part of the island is named after the village in which it is located.

Hidden within the trees is this community library, housed in a log cabin in the forest.

The route around the island is 55 miles (88 km) long and follows the coast.

ABOVE

The ferry takes an hour to reach the Isle of Arran from Ardrossan, just to the west of Glasgow.

OPPOSITE

The island is well known as being Scotland in miniature, at least in terms of its scenery.

ABOVE

Groups of seals can often be seen off the west coast.

OPPOSITE

The view from Lagg in the south of the island takes in a coastline of varying terrain and constantly shifting light from the sea.

DEEP DIVE

MAKING WHISKY

The making of whisky (Scotch) is integral to Scotland and part of the nation's history. It is made in five main whisky-producing regions, from the Isle of Islay to Speyside—a very special spirit that has left its mark on both the landscape and the local culture.

"Scotch whisky is more than a whisky. It is part of Scotland's heritage and folklore." It was with these words uttered in the UK Parliament in 1987 that member of parliament Bill Walker summed up the connection between the "amber nectar" and the nation of Scotland. Known as *uisge beatha* ("water of life") in Gaelic, the origins of whisky are thought to date back to the fourth or fifth century and the arrival of monks from Europe who brought with them their distilling techniques and Christianity.

The first record of distilling was in 1494, when King James IV commanded friar John Cor of Lindores Abbey to produce *aqua vitae.* The imposition of government duty on whisky production in 1644 resulted in a boom in the number of illicit stills, and by the end of the eighteenth century, there were around four hundred bootleg distilleries compared with just a dozen legal ones. These circumstances were mitigated in 1823 with the Excise Act, which eased restrictions on distillery licensing and marked the birth of the modern industry. The Scotch Whisky Association (SWA) recorded one hundred and fifty-two distilleries in operation in Scotland in 2025.

To be recognized as true Scotch whisky, the spirit has to be distilled in Scotland from three ingredients only (water, yeast, and grains), aged in oak casks for a minimum of three years, and have an alcohol content of at least forty percent ABV. Scotch is divided into five categories: single malt Scotch (made from malted barley in a single distillery); single grain Scotch (distilled from various grains in a single distillery); blended Scotch (a mixture of single malts and single grains from multiple distilleries); blended malt Scotch (a mixture of single malts from multiple distilleries); and blended grain Scotch (a mixture of single grain whiskies from multiple distilleries).

Five regions are involved in making Scotch, with each adding their own unique touch to the bottles they produce: Islay, Campbeltown, Lowland, Highland, and Speyside. More than half of all the distilleries in the country are to be found in the last of these, so it is an ideal starting point for exploring this amber-colored spirit. Speyside whiskies are famous for their elegance and sophistication, with subtle notes of hazelnuts and fruit. That said, connoisseurs are also encouraged to venture off the beaten track and seek out smaller independent distilleries—and to discover a little of the soul of Scotland as they do so.

THE WHISKY PRODUCTION CYCLE

01

MALTING

Germinating the barley
in preparation.

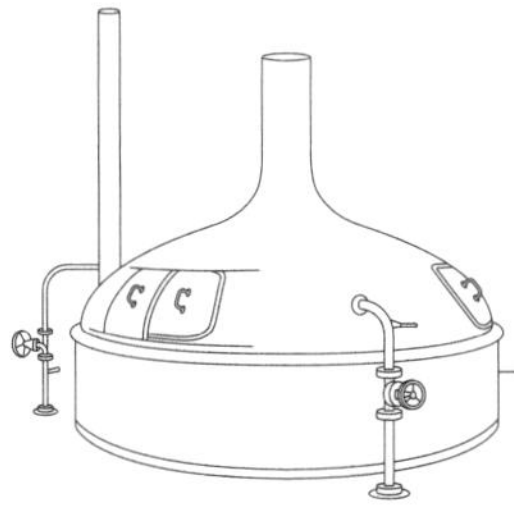

02

MASHING

Extracting the sugars required
for fermentation.

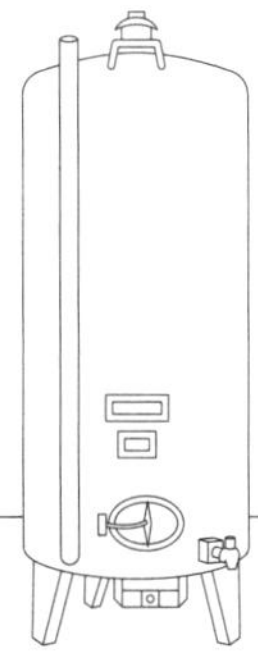

03

FERMENTATION

Transforming the sugars
into alcohol.

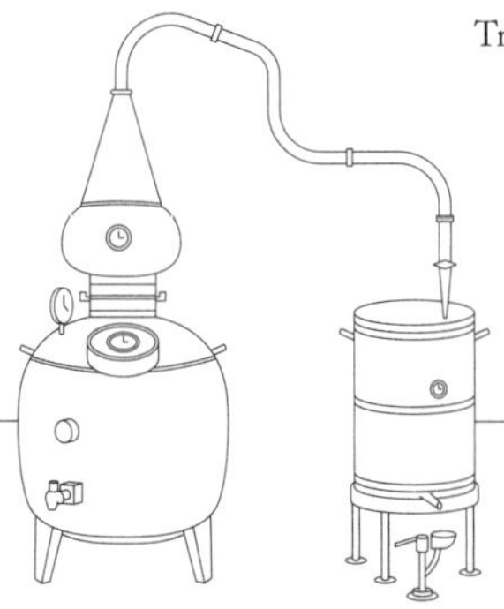

04

DISTILLATION

Separating the alcohol
and water.

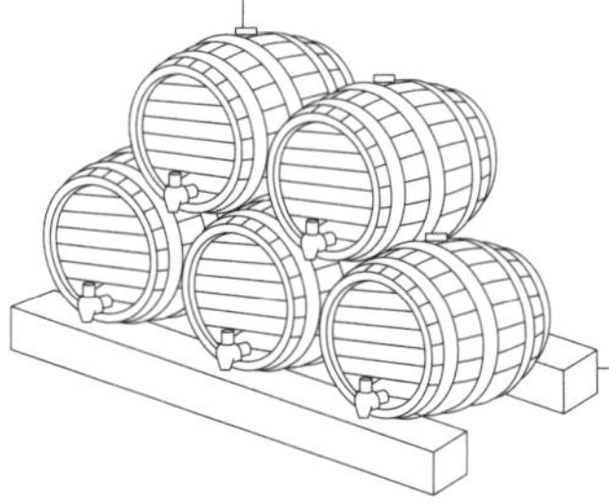

05

MATURATION

Stabilizing and refining the
flavor profile.

06

BOTTLING

Conditioning for drinking.

ABOVE

This distillery founded just north of Glasgow in 1833 makes a virtue of slow maturation, with whiskies aged for up to thirty years.

OPPOSITE

The barrels require six years of seasoning and are custom-made from oak.

GLENGOYNE DISTILLERY
DUMGOYNE
GLENGOYNE DISTILLERY
LANG BROS Ltd
DUMGOYNE
247
1995
499
GLENGOYNE DISTILLERY
DUMGOYNE
247
2006
2417
GLENGOYNE DISTILLERY
DUMGOYNE
2011
1740
GLENGOYNE DISTILLERY
1984
1567
GLENGOYNE DISTILLERY
LANG BROS Ltd
DUMGOYNE
484
1972
3310

VISIT

GLASGOW BOTANIC GARDENS

AN ICONIC LOCATION

Glasgow Botanic Gardens were founded in 1817 and have been part of the cityscape for more than two hundred years. The University of Glasgow was also involved in establishing and developing the gardens.

THOMAS HOPKIRK

Thomas Hopkirk was the botanist behind the creation of the gardens.

A CLASSICAL FIGURE

A classical sculpture emerges from the backdrop of ferns and exotic shrubs.

A WIDE COLLECTION

The glasshouse is a riot of orchids, carnivorous plants, and cacti.

TROPICAL GLASSHOUSES

Ferns and carnivorous plants thrive in the humid atmosphere of the Victorian glasshouses, which recreate conditions similar to those in tropical zones.

IRON AND GLASS

The Kibble Palace is a glasshouse commissioned by John Kibble. Built in 1871 it was moved to the gardens in 1873 and houses a collection of tree ferns and tropical plants.

CROWNING GLORY

The Victorian glasshouse is topped with a cupola made of glass and metal.

TEMPERATE ZONE

There is an interplay of textures and materials in the iron and glass framework.

ARCHITECTURE

The iron and glass enclosure provides protection for plants growing in temperate zones.

Loch Lomond & The Trossachs, Scotland's first national park, marks the border between the Highlands and Lowlands.

In summer sheep graze on the slopes of Conic Hill beside Loch Lomond.

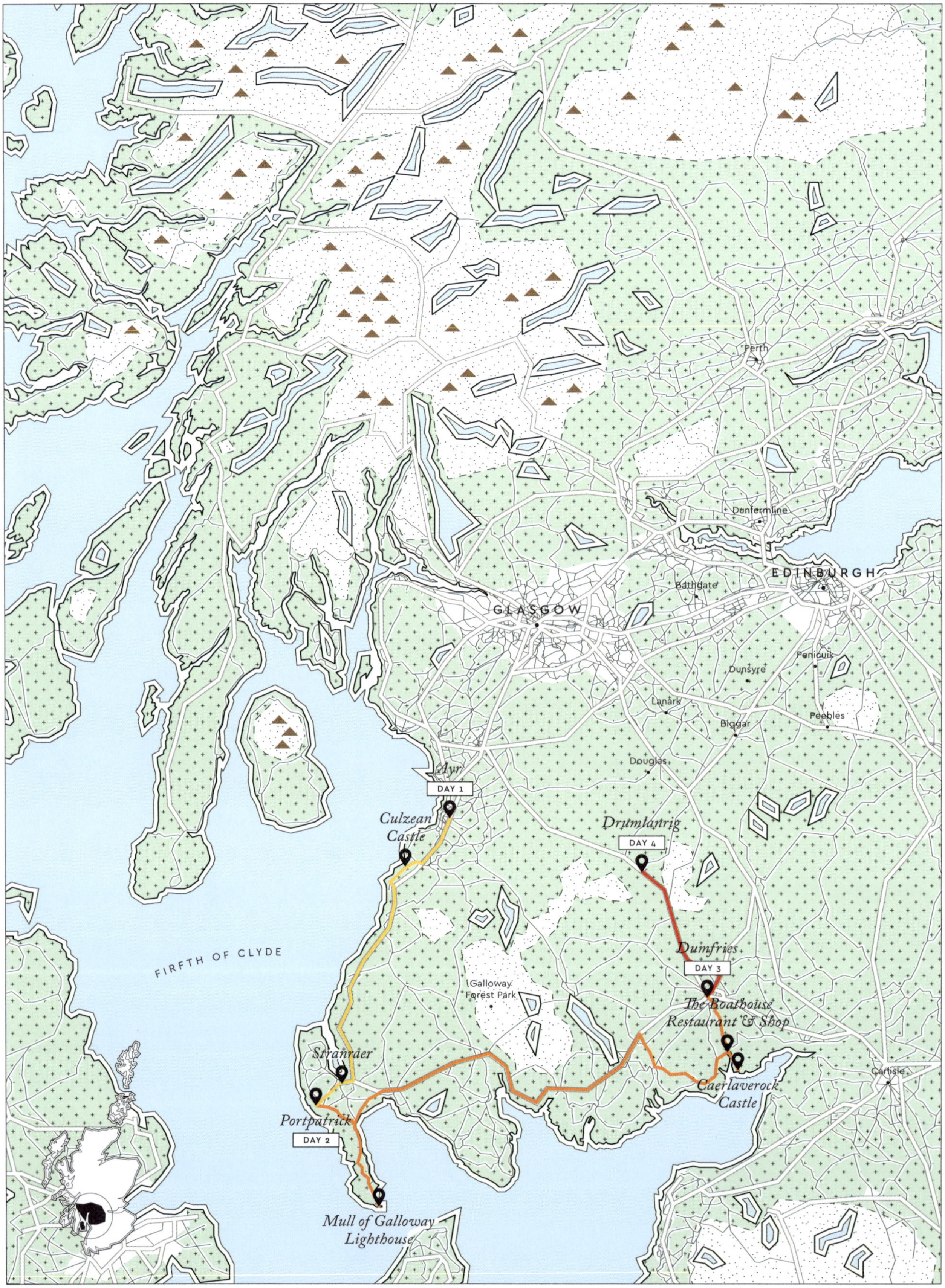
Perth
Dunfermline
EDINBURGH
Bathgate
GLASGOW
Penicuik
Dunsyre
Lanark
Biggar
Peebles
Douglas
Ayr
DAY 1
Culzean Castle
Drumlanrig
DAY 4
FIRTH OF CLYDE
Dumfries
DAY 3
Galloway Forest Park
The Boathouse Restaurant & Shop
Stranraer
Carlisle
Caerlaverock Castle
Portpatrick
DAY 2
Mull of Galloway Lighthouse

EXCURSION

FOUR DAYS SOUTH OF GLASGOW

The region of Dumfries and Galloway to the south of Glasgow is still a well-kept secret. Extending from the Irish Sea to the Borders, the scenery ranges from jagged cliffs to lush forests and remote hills, and the whole area is scattered with majestic abbeys and photogenic castle ruins.

DAY 1: BESIDE THE IRISH SEA

The coast road from Ayr to Stranraer skirts the cliffs looking out over the Irish Sea. Standing proudly on a headland is Culzean Castle, a pleasing blend of medieval fortress and sophisticated, late-eighteenth century interiors arranged around an oval staircase designed by the architect Robert Adam. At 299 square miles (774 km^2), Galloway Forest Park, a little further east, is the largest forest park in the United Kingdom. The scenery here offers a small foretaste of the Highlands. With skies free from light pollution, the park is particularly popular with fans of astronomy as it is an ideal place for stargazing.

DAY 2: MULL OF GALLOWAY

Look out for the colorful cottages of the small fishing port of Portpatrick on the way to the peninsula known as the Rhins of Galloway. Follow the coastal road at the southern end to find a hiking trail leading to the clifftop ruin of Dunskey Castle overlooking the sea. On reaching the windswept cliffs of the peninsula's southernmost tip (and the most southerly tip of Scotland itself), it might feel as though you have reached the ends of the earth. This is also the location of the Mull of Galloway Lighthouse established in 1830 by Robert Stevenson of the Lighthouse Stevensons, the dynasty of civil engineers who built many of Scotland's lighthouses. The nearby Gallie Craig Coffee House offers sustenance while looking out to sea for guillemots, dolphins, and porpoises.

DAY 3: DUMFRIES

The Boathouse Restaurant & Shop on the way to Dumfries makes a welcome stop. This bistro on the banks of the River Nith has made a real name for itself with its food—especially brunch—and its store crammed full of local produce. Caerlaverock Castle lies just before Dumfries (the largest town in the area), another medieval fortress. Dumfries' red sandstone bridges make it easy to get around this former royal burgh nicknamed the Queen of the South (also the name of the town's soccer team). Dumfries is closely associated with Robert Burns (1759–1796), the national poet of Scotland, who spent his last years here.

DAY 4: DRUMLANRIG CASTLE

Making your way back north, the Nithsdale countryside now spreads out before you, where a fine castle of rose-colored stone stands in the middle of nearly 7,500 acres (30,000 ha) of grounds. Drumlanrig Castle was built in the seventeenth century and artfully combines traditional corner turrets with Renaissance elements. Inside is an impressive collection of paintings, including *An Old Woman Reading* by Rembrandt. The gardens laid out in the French style round off both this visit and tour off the beaten track.

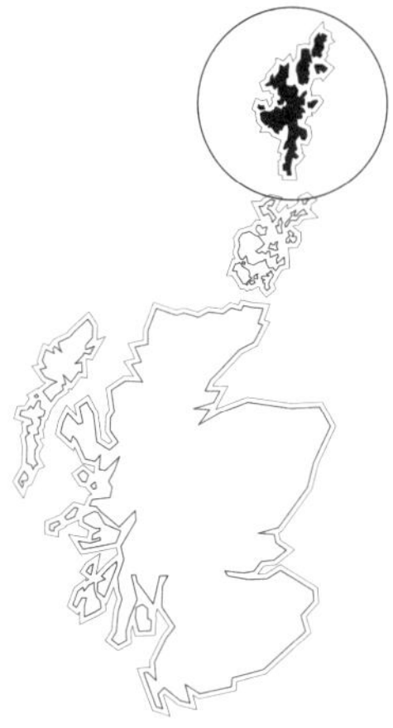

BETWEEN SCOTLAND AND SCANDINAVIA

SHETLAND

The Shetland Islands, almost equidistant between Scotland and Norway, have a unique identity that blends Scottish and Nordic cultures.

P.226

The remains of a house near the volcanic fissures at Eshaness. Around twenty-three thousand people live in Shetland.

OPPOSITE

Ruins near the Muckle Roe Lighthouse on the west coast of Shetland. The island of Papa Stour can just be glimpsed on the horizon.

This is a magnificent region, seemingly lost between the Atlantic Ocean and the North Sea. Lying some 100 miles (160 km) off the coast of mainland Scotland, Shetland consists of around one hundred islands, sixteen of which are inhabited. Some historians maintain it is the island of Thule that the Greek geographer Pytheas claimed to have seen in the fourth century BCE.

With around 1,700 miles (2,700 km) of jagged coastline, the islands are entirely at the mercy of the sea, which also dictates everything from the weather to the islands' economy and the inhabitants' way of life. It is possible to reach Shetland by plane, but access is generally by ferry boat. Despite the twelve- to fourteen-hour crossing required from Aberdeen, the trip to the islands is more than worthwhile, if only to see the striking landscapes created by geological activity that began several million years ago. Shetland is as close to the North Pole as Alaska or Greenland, but the North Atlantic Drift (an offshoot of the Gulf Stream) brings warm water from the Gulf of Mexico, keeping the surrounding sea ice-free all year round. As a result, there is a wide variety of flora and fauna, some of which are unique to the islands, including Shetland ponies, colonies of puffins and Northern gannets, and the minke whales, orca, and fin whales that can be found in the coastal waters. The earliest traces of human activity date back some six thousand years—Shetland has been inhabited in turn by Celts, Picts, and Vikings, all of whom left archeological traces of their occupation. The archipelago was colonized and ruled by Norway for more than six centuries, and its language and traditions have been deeply influenced by the customs of the eastern extremes of the countries bordering the North Sea.

In 1469 the king of Denmark and Norway promised the islands of Orkney and Shetland as his daughter Margaret's dowry upon her marriage to King James III of Scotland. Although Denmark later tried to reclaim the islands, which had in effect been pawned to James III, they were eventually permanently integrated into Scotland. They nevertheless retained a culture that was both Scottish and Nordic. For proof of this, look no further than the Up Helly Aa Fire Festival, inspired by Viking tradition and held every year between January and March. The island communities come together for the night to parade with torches and to dance to traditional Shetland music. The Northern Lights have sometimes been known to put in an appearance on such occasions too.

THE ESSENTIALS

HERMANESS NATIONAL NATURE RESERVE

The moorland of Unst comes to an abrupt end at Hermaness with the northernmost cliffs in the United Kingdom, home to vast colonies of Atlantic seabirds.

68

JARLSHOF

Evidence of more than four thousand years of human habitation, from the Bronze Age to the sixteenth century, is found in Shetland's South Mainland.

69

ESHANESS

The fissures created by volcanic activity in Eshaness form some of the most impressive scenery on the islands.

70

ISLE OF NOSS

This national nature reserve, where thousands of seabirds nest on its spectacular cliffs, can be reached via a short boat trip in summer.

71

SUMBURGH HEAD LIGHTHOUSE

Built at the southern tip of the islands by Robert Stevenson in 1821, this is the oldest lighthouse in Shetland.

72

MUCKLE ROE LIGHTHOUSE

A hiking path leads to this lighthouse on Muckle Roe, an island famous for its cliffs of red granite.

73

LERWICK

The island capital was all about the herring trade until the nineteenth century. It now boasts some beautiful Victorian homes and an attractive shopping street.

ABOVE

A vast colony of Northern gannets make their home on Hermaness National Nature Reserve on the northern tip of Shetland.

OPPOSITE

The reserve teems with birds; there are some thirty thousand pairs of Northern gannets here alone.

ABOVE

Sweeping coastal views on St Ninian's Isle, where eighth-century Pictish treasure was discovered in a ruined chapel, now displayed in the National Museum of Scotland, Edinburgh.

OPPOSITE

St Ninian's Isle is connected to Shetland's Mainland by a wide "tombolo," a natural isthmus of sand.

NATURE

BREEDING SHETLAND PONIES

A handful of horse breeders on the Shetland Islands are ensuring the survival of the Shetland pony, an iconic breed that originated here several millennia ago.

Carol Fullerton's house stands high on a hill to the north of Scalloway, looking out over the meadow where her ponies graze. Twenty-six mares and six stallions make up the core of her herd, to which several foals are added each year. Breeding Shetland ponies is a tradition for the female members of Carol's family—following in the footsteps of her mother and grandmother, Carol is the third generation to raise this island breed on these windswept hills.

The history of the breed is closely entwined with the history of the islands. The ponies' presence here has been documented since the Bronze Age (with their bones discovered at the Jarlshof prehistoric site) but it is highly likely that they were already living on Shetland as long as four thousand years ago. Their hardy nature reflects the harshness of the surroundings in which they have evolved, complemented by a process of natural selection that has been in operation for centuries, with only the strongest individuals being able to survive. Standing less than 11 hands (1.07 m) high at the withers, they are among the smallest ponies on the British Isles, but they are more than able to thrive and survive here on the marshy moorland, peat bogs, and rocky hills.

The absence of proper roads until the nineteenth century meant that crofters (farmers who subsisted from both fishing and agriculture) would use the ponies to transport peat, manure, and even seaweed, but the Industrial Revolution was to have a hand in their fate. In 1842 the United Kingdom passed the Mines and Collieries Act prohibiting women and girls, and boys under ten, from working underground, and the subsequent surge in demand for Shetland ponies lasted until the 1960s.

While the population of Shetland ponies on the islands has dwindled from its nineteenth-century high point of ten thousand to just over a thousand today, the breed has spread far beyond its homeland. Ponies began to be exported to the Netherlands in the seventeenth century, soon followed by America, and there are now more than one hundred thousand ponies scattered across all four corners of the earth. The Shetland Pony Stud Book Society was created in 1890 to regulate and preserve the breed and to maintain a genealogical record, and each pony is now required to have a passport that records its precise pedigree—one way of ensuring that the links to their homeland are never forgotten.

PASSPORT

Every Shetland pony has a passport issued by the Shetland Pony Stud Book Society.

IN GOOD COMPANY

The ponies may once have been used to haul peat or coal, but they are now highly prized as companion animals.

ABOVE

An archeological project on the island of Unst has excavated three Viking longhouses; the one shown here is a replica.

OPPOSITE

The Skíðblaðnir, a reproduction of a Viking drakkar (a type of longship) can be seen just south of Haroldswick.

ARCHEOLOGY

JARLSHOF

The archeological site at Jarlshof spans four thousand years of human history, from the Bronze Age, Iron Age, and Norse communities of the medieval era, to the seventeenth century.

Lying in the south of Shetland's main island (known as Mainland) and looking out over the West Voe Beach of Sumburgh bay, Jarlshof is one of those places whose importance is not immediately apparent. An initial examination of its windswept stone walls, wild grassland, and the sea below would never suggest that more than four millennia of human life have been lived out here. A violent storm in the 1890s uncovered the site that had been lying hidden beneath the sand dunes and was followed by excavation work that continued into the mid-twentieth century. The remains of a Bronze Age village thought to date as far back as around 2700 BCE were discovered as well as a *broch*, a conical dry-stone tower, and wheelhouses from the Iron Age (500 BCE onward), a collection of Viking longhouses and outbuildings, and even a seventeenth-century Scottish dwelling—to walk across the site is literally to travel through time.

Several of the wheelhouses are perfectly preserved apart from their roofs and were a unique find in Scotland. The term "wheelhouse" derives from the walls that radiate out from a central hearth like the spokes of a wheel. They supported the roof, which would have been made of layers of turf. Stepping inside, it is easy to imagine how these thick walls protected those within from storms, with a central fire and some oil lamps their only sources of heat and light.

The rectangular longhouses nearby are evidence of a Viking presence. Having arrived from Western Norway around 850 CE, they adapted their Scandinavian architecture (which used wood) to the harshness of the Shetland climate. With no timber to work with, they built dwellings by stacking up layers of stones and covering them with turf and grass. The thick walls provided shelter for families, stables, and a forge. The site was therefore more a large farm than a village, a self-sufficient settlement beside the wild sea.

The Old House of Sumburgh (also known as the Laird's House), is the most recent ruin on the site (built in the 1500s, later fortified, then modernized in the seventeenth century), and tells the tale of the end of an era. Shetland had long been the property of the kingdom of Denmark and Norway but was annexed to Scotland in 1469 when King Christian I gave it in dowry to his daughter Margaret upon her marriage to King James III of Scotland. Power was then handed to Robert Stewart, First Earl of Orkney, and in the early seventeenth century, Robert's son Patrick Stewart, nicknamed "Black Patie" for his cruelty, modernized the Old House of Sumburgh which still dominates the site today. Two centuries later, Sir Walter Scott took it as inspiration for his novel *The Pirate* and gave the site its current name—Jarlshof means "the earl's mansion."

1 / WHEELHOUSE

The entrance to one of the best-preserved Iron Age wheelhouses in Scotland.

2 / 3 / NATURE

Nature is busy reclaiming this archeological site that has been left open to the elements.

4 / CONTINUITY

Jarlshof is still being studied by archeologists more than a century after its discovery.

5 / RELICS

Thousands of items have been excavated, providing evidence of the daily routines and personal and spiritual lives of the inhabitants.

ABOVE

The natural scenery just a stone's throw from the center of Lerwick, the capital of the islands, is magnificent.

OPPOSITE

The Knab is rocky headland with breathtaking panoramic views of the sea.

DEEP DIVE

THE STEVENSON DYNASTY

From the southern tip of Dumfries and Galloway to the distant coastline of Shetland, no less than two hundred and eight lighthouses guide seafarers safely through fog, tides, and storms. More than half of these marvels of engineering were designed by the Stevenson family.

It all began with the birth of a son, Robert, to sugar merchant Alan Stevenson and his wife Jean Lillie Stevenson in Glasgow on 8 June 1772. Alan Stevenson was to die of a fever in the Caribbean two years later, and his widow remarried several years after that, wedding Thomas Smith, an accomplished mechanic who had been appointed as an engineer to the newly instituted Northern Lighthouse Board (NLB). This organization had been established in 1786 with a view to improving the safety of the sea off Scotland's coasts by constructing lighthouses.

Thomas took Robert under his wing and employed him as an apprentice. They worked together to oversee construction of the Little Cumbrae Lighthouse on the Firth of Clyde. Robert was only nineteen at the time, but his destiny was now sealed forever. He went on to work as an engineer for the Northern Lighthouse Board for almost half a century and was involved in the construction of seventeen lighthouses, not to mention the numerous projects to which he contributed without being in direct charge. Robert's masterpiece remains the Bell Rock Lighthouse, built on a notoriously dangerous reef just off the Angus coast. The rock is accessible only at low tide and it took sixty laborers more than three years to complete the work. Thanks to the robustness of its design, the lighthouse has remained in perfect shape to this day.

Robert was also the inventor a system of flashing and intermittent lights, an innovation for which he was awarded a gold medal by the king of the Netherlands. His work inspired three of his sons (David, Alan, and Thomas) to follow in his footsteps and join the Northern Lighthouse Board. The three brothers supervised the construction of more than forty lighthouses in total, from Dunnet Head, the northernmost point of mainland Britain, to Skerryvore, a lighthouse built from Mull granite on a rocky island off the west coast. At 157 ft (48 m) and with one hundred and fifty-one steps, the lighthouse is the tallest in Scotland.

The next chapter in the family's history was written by David's two sons, Charles and David Alan, who carried on the family tradition into the 1930s and cooperated on the design of more than ninety lighthouses. Robert Stevenson and his descendants were therefore the builders of many of Scotland's lighthouses for some one hundred and fifty years, ensuring their names were part of the country's history. Thomas's only son, Robert Louis Stevenson, chose a very different path and became an author. As a novelist and travel writer, he left behind a much celebrated body of work that includes *Treasure Island*, *Travels with a Donkey in the Cévennes*, and *The Strange Case of Dr. Jekyll and Mr. Hyde*. His poem entitled "The Lightkeeper" is less well known, but may have been a small nod to his ancestors.

A NETWORK OF LIGHTHOUSES

REMARKABLE LIGHTHOUSES

1 Skerryvore 2 Dunnet Head 3 Little Cumbrae 4 Bell Rock

* other lighthouses

LANDMARKS FOR NAVIGATION

Scottish lighthouses mark the position of coasts, channels, and submerged sand and gravel banks. Their location is determined by precise criteria for visibility, luminous range, and alignment, to ensure they can guide vessels in what are often very difficult conditions.

ABOVE

Sumburgh Head at the southernmost tip of Shetland is an ideal place for bird watching and spotting marine mammals.

OPPOSITE

Puffins are most likely to be seen between the months of April and August.

EXPEDITION

SHETLAND SEABIRD TOUR

OBSERVATION

Naturalist Phil Harris and photographer Rebecca Nason offer special tours for spotting seabirds from Lerwick.

NATURALIST

Phil Harris has been living on Shetland for more than twenty years.

FISH

A bucket of fish ready for northern gannets, expert divers reaching speeds of up to 60 mph (100 km/h).

NORTHERN GANNETS

A colony of Northern gannets nests on the cliffs between May and September.

ISLE OF NOSS

Catching a first glimpse of the cliffs of the Isle of Noss, reached only by boat.

LOCAL FISHING

A lobster boat off the coast of the Isle of Noss.

LERWICK HARBOR

Many boat excursions leave from Lerwick, which is the capital of the islands.

GREAT SKUA

Skuas, the large predatory seabirds also known as bonxies, rule the these waters.

RECORD-BREAKING

The Northern gannet is the largest seabird in the world and can dive from heights of 100 ft (30 m) to catch fish underwater.

ABOVE

The church of Dunrossness in the southern part of Mainland.

OPPOSITE

Hjaltland, the Old Norse name for Shetland, is said to derive from the islands' shape, which reminded the Vikings of a sword hilt (hjalt).

ABOVE

Shetland place names are a reminder of six hundred years of Norwegian rule.

OPPOSITE

The islands lie in a unique position in almost the same latitudes as Bergen in Norway and the southern tip of Greenland.

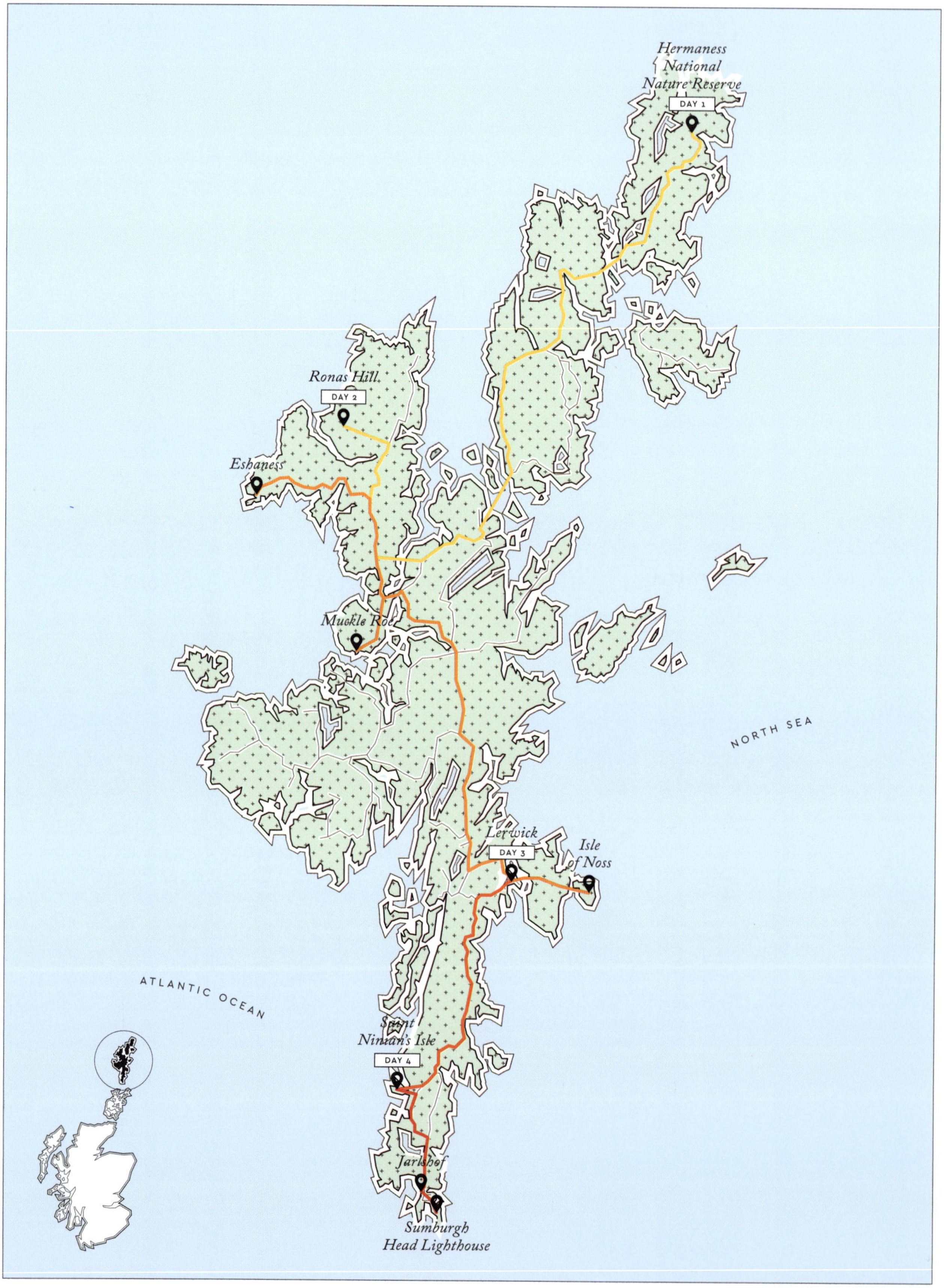
Hermaness
National
Nature Reserve
DAY 1
Ronas Hill
DAY 2
Eshaness
Muckle Roe
NORTH SEA
Lerwick
DAY 3
Isle
of Noss
ATLANTIC OCEAN
Saint
Ninian's Isle
DAY 4
Jarlshof
Sumburgh
Head Lighthouse

EXCURSION

SHETLAND FROM NORTH TO SOUTH

Shetland is a wild and windswept archipelago lying far to the north of Scotland where the North Atlantic meets the North Sea. Its steep cliffs, remote beaches, moors and lochs, and narrow roads winding between hills give visitors the impression of being at the edge of the world.

DAY 1: UNST

The northernmost outpost of the British Isles feels completely isolated. In summer the heather-covered moors and steep cliffs of Hermaness National Nature Reserve are home to thousands of seabirds, including Northern gannets, guillemots, and puffins. From the top of the cliffs, the view stretches to Muckle Flugga Lighthouse on its wave-battered rock.

DAY 2: NORTH MAINLAND

Further south the landscape becomes rocky. The basalt columns emerging from the sea at Eshaness are evidence of previous volcanic activity, and the wind howls between the black cliffs where the ocean comes crashing in. Ronas Hill is the highest point in Shetland with a spectacular view of the surrounding lochs and moorland. The attractive island of Muckle Roe with its rugged terrain, red sandstone coves, and paths through the heather, lies further south still.

DAY 3: LERWICK AND THE ISLE OF NOSS

On the way to Lerwick, Shetland's busy capital, fishing boats can be seen moored in the harbor, which is lined with stone cottages. Explore its small streets to find cafés and artisan stores. The Isle of Noss, just beyond the island of Bressay, is a sanctuary for seabirds, and during the nesting season the cliffs turn into living walls of thousands of gannets. Join a boat trip around Noss from Lerwick and you might find yourself being escorted by seals.

DAY 4: THE SOUTHERN PART OF THE ISLAND

The scenery softens, becoming less dramatic toward the south part of Shetland. A strip of golden sand connects St Ninian's Isle to Mainland, forming one of the most spectacular tombolos (natural sand causeways) in Europe. Further south still, the archeological site at Jarlshof reveals four thousand years of human history, from Neolithic dwellings to a seventeenth-century nobleman's house. The road comes to an end at Sumburgh Head, where a lighthouse stands on top of cliffs teeming with puffins, and it is here, facing the wind and the waves, that the true wild beauty of Shetland reveals itself.

BIOGRAPHY

Paris-born journalist and photographer Maud Simon files reports from France and all over the world. Her work combines the journalistic elements of documentary with a strong esthetic sense inspired by cinematography. In capturing their natural beauty, she strives to convey an authentic vision of the regions she visits and their inhabitants.

I would like to thank the whole team at Éditions du Chêne, and Emmanuel Le Vallois, Sabine Houplain, and Faris Issad in particular, for their continuing faith in me and their keen attention to detail. Thank you to Bureau Berger for their artistic direction and to Franck Friès and Mireille Touret for having the eyes of a lynx. A final round of thanks is due to Orson and Scott for their routinely cheery support.

PHOTOGRAPHIC CREDITS

All the photographs in this book are by Maud Simon, with the exception of:
© Florian Fuchs/CC BY 3.0: 75; © Ian Rutherford/Alamy Image Bank: 12; © John Mcmillan/Unsplash: 168; © Liam Riby/Unsplash: 169; © MichaelGrant/Alamy Image Bank: 105; © Miraxh Tereziu/Unsplash: 43; © Neil Bussey/Alamy Image Bank: 137; © Pascal Bullan/Unsplash: 137; © Peter Moore / CC BY-SA 2.0: 137; © Rico Meier/Unsplash: 43; © Thom Frijns/Unsplash: 137; © Thomas Andy Branson/CC BY-SA 4.0: 105; © Tim Woolliscroft/Unsplash: 75; © UrbanImages/Alamy Image Bank: 105.

First published in English in 2026
by Rizzoli Universe, a division of
Rizzoli International Publications

Rizzoli International Publications Inc
49 West 27th Street
New York, NY 10001

Rizzoli International Publications UK Ltd
Somerset House, West Wing
Strand, London WC2R 1LA

www.rizzoliusa.com

Originally published in French in 2026 as
Petit Atlas Hédoniste – Écosse by © 2026,
Éditions du Chêne – Hachette Livre
www.editionsduchene.fr

For Rizzoli
Publisher: Charles Miers
Associate Publisher: Tina Persaud
Senior Editor: Kristy Richardson

For Éditions du Chêne
Editor-in chief: Emmanuel Le Vallois
Artistic director: Sabine Houplain

ISBN 978-07893-4686-5

2026 / 1
Printed in China

The authorized representative in the EU for safety and compliance is Mondadori Libri S.p.A., via Gian Battista Vico 42, Milan, Italy, 0123, www.mondadori.it

Visit us online: Instagram.com/RizzoliBooks
Facebook.com/RizzoliNewYork
Youtube.com/user/RizzoliNY

FSC www.fsc.org
MIX
Paper | Supporting responsible forestry
FSC® C104723